JOHN D. FLYNN

&

GAYLORDSVILLE
HISTORICAL SOCIETY

JOHN D. FLYNN

&

GAYLORDSVILLE
HISTORICAL SOCIETY

JOHN D. FLYNN

To order additional copies of this book, contact:
Xlibris
1-888-795-4274
www.Xlibris.com
Orders@Xlibris.com
538716

This fourth edition of the
History of Gaylordsville
is dedicated to
John D. Flynn

Made possible by
The Gaylordsville Historical Society

First Printing January 1974
Second Printing March 1974
Third Printing June 1989
Fourth Printing Spring 2016
Fifth Printing Fall 2016

John Flynn as a teenager at Numeral Rock in Kent

FOREWORD

The reprinting of this book has been a most challenging and delightful experience for me. I was so very fortunate to work with some dedicated volunteer editors, willing to donate whatever time was necessary to make this revision a reality.

Reading through the writings of John Flynn really showed the love he had for this community. To do what he did was a major endeavor: to publish a book about the place where he grew up and lived his life. This fourth edition is filled with the same writings that John Flynn initially published along with some updated sections and pictures that continue to depict Gaylordsville's history through the present day. We decided to add a table of contents, chapter titles and an index, to assist the reader in locating specific areas of interest within the book.

The Gaylordsville Historical Society is most appreciative to the Flynn family, especially Aline and Peter, for their generous gesture in allowing us to republish and distribute this book. Ironically, since the book went out-of-print a few years back, the Historical Society has received numerous requests for copies of it. Fortunately, through the wonders of modern electronic publishing, this book will never go out of print again. Furthermore, because of this current technology, future revisions of this book can be made quite easily. Suggestions for future revisions can always be made to the Gaylordsville Historical Society through our website at www.gaylordsville.org, as we welcome your thoughts and ideas.

In closing, I would like to thank Barbara Thorland for her perseverance in having a book revision committee formed and working diligently to ensure everything that needed to be revised or added to, was accomplished. Many thanks to the late Mimi Burkhardt for all of the hours of reading, revising and adding information to this book. There were also many others who, throughout the process of revising this manuscript, offered their assistance that ultimately helped the individual committee members accomplish their goals. To them I offer heartfelt thanks. Finally, to Joan Brothers, the person who read through each and every word, sentence, page and chapter of this book, time and time again to make sure everything was "just right", I offer my sincere thanks and gratitude.

To the reader, I hope you truly enjoy this edition of John Flynn's History of Gaylordsville, Connecticut.

Richard T. Kosier, President
Gaylordsville Historical Society

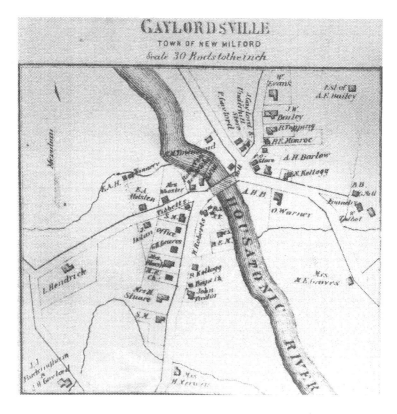

GAYLORDVILLE'S HISTORY

The early history of Gaylordsville is closely connected to the Gaylord family, or Gaillard, as the family was known in France. In 1630 William Gaylord arrived in Nantucket harbor on the ship "Mary and John", which had sailed from Plymouth, England. He later settled in East Windsor, Connecticut. His great-grandson, Ensign William Gaylord, moved to Woodbury in 1706 and married Joanna, the daughter of Captain John Minor. Joanna's sister, Grace, married Samuel Grant, who was an ancestor of President Grant.

In 1712, the Gaylord couple came to New Milford, Connecticut, which had been settled only five years previously. Their house stood on the corner of Main and Elm Streets. For a time he kept a tavern there in addition to doing his regular work as a surveyor. He did a lot of surveying for the state, laying out town boundary lines. It was, no doubt, on one of these surveying trips that he became impressed with the large areas of level land several miles north of the New Milford village, just north of the straits on the Housatonic River. He began taking title to parcels of it, and soon owned a large part of the valley. To insure the good will of the Indians living in the area, he also bought land from them, giving, according to legend, a horse, a mule, and a two-wheeled cart.

In 1722, a highway was laid out "by marked trees" north from New Milford to the brook called Whemiseck. The blazed trail ran through Squash Hollow, past the straits, and over Cedar Hill. Mr. Gaylord was probably the surveyor who laid out this road, and probably put it over Cedar Hill so it would not cut into the level areas that were to become his fields.

In 1725, Mr. Gaylord traveled this trail from New Milford and built a log cabin west of the Housatonic just north of the straits. He lived in this cabin three years while he was clearing land, cutting timbers, and building his frame house, which he built in 1728. The following year his oldest son, Aaron, built a house about a quarter of a mile south of his father's home on the west side of the valley.

During this time the Gaylord family became good friends with their Indian neighbors, teaching them better methods of agriculture and dickering with them for furs they could use. The family consisted of Mr. and Mrs. Gaylord, Aaron, Joanna, Ruth, Benjamin, and Mary. Benjamin remained at his father's home and eventually took over the homestead. He married Tryal Morehouse on October 23, 1745.

William Gaylord died October 25, 1743, at the age of 73. His grave and that of Mrs. Gaylord were the first ones in a cemetery that had been laid out about half a mile south of the Gaylord home.

Gaylord Home Built in 1728-Picture taken in 1905
when the home was owned by Fremont Hall

George Washington had his noon meal here on September 20, 1780. He was on his way to Hartford with his staff and escort to consult with the Count de Rochambeau and the other French officers who were as yet not committed to helping the Continental Army in the fight for independence. Great things were hoped for from this conference.

The journey had been planned and all arrangements made for each stopping place by couriers sent out previously, and these agents had decided on the route from headquarters at Tappan on the Hudson, through Peekskill, Fishkill, Gaylordsville, and Litchfield, instead of through Danbury and Woodbury as at first intended.

The roads were poor, many of them mere bridle trails. Good mounts were essential. Most of the men in Washington's party owned their horses and had been picked for the trip because of their excellent horses. They arrived in Gaylordsville by way of the Dover Road, now called Newton Road, which came right to a large oak tree not far from the Gaylord home. The men rested under the tree and ate their lunch while General Washington, his aide, the Marquis de Lafayette, and one or two other officers, dined with Deacon Benjamin Gaylord, with whom Washington was already acquainted. Following their meal, the General and his staff held a conference under the tree before continuing on their journey.

The Washington Oak gradually deteriorated and finally came crashing down in 2003. The Connecticut DAR planted another oak tree in 2007.

Legend tells us that Washington again passed through here in May 1781 and no doubt again paused under the oak. At a still later date, Lafayette made the trip by himself, and was entertained overnight in the Gaylord home. The room he occupied was a source of pride to the owners as long as the house stood, and still had the fine paneling which was quite unusual in a house built in the wilderness in the early seventeen hundreds.

The residents of Gaylord's Village during the Revolution were a patriotic group. The old cemetery contains the graves of six who served in the Army. They were Nathaniel Terry, Jonathan Giddings, Ebenezer Gaylord, Peter Waller, Nathaniel Osborn, and Zephaniah Briggs. The men who could not leave to join the Army formed a vigilante group to guard against the Tories. They surprised a group of Tories in a cave about a mile south of the village and took a quantity of guns, ammunition and other supplies that were hidden there. The cave was later called Tories Cave, and is still known by that name. When the American flag came into being, the women of the village got together and made a flag. It was flown daily on a hill top east of the river. This is still known as Liberty Hill, and was used as a picnic ground for many years.

Gaylordsville is located in the northwest corner of New Milford. It is part of the valley known to the Indians as Wemanesa or Red Plumb Plain. On the East the boundary is Quanuctnic or Long Mountain, but it has never been decided whether that boundary should be at the foot of the mountain or somewhere up on top. The southern boundary is also vague, usually considered to be an imaginary line leaving the Housatonic River somewhere south of Tories Cave and extending across Squash Hollow. The Sherman town line forms the Western boundary, although several homes in Sherman are usually considered to be part of the Gaylordsville community.

The Housatonic River runs through the center of the village and is joined by the Wimisink, Womunshenuck, Naromiyocknowhusunkatankshunk, and Squash Hollow brooks. The south end of the valley is divided into two narrow valleys by Strait's Mountain or Pauguiack. The north end of this overlooks the village and is called "The Pinnacle." The area usually considered to be Gaylordsville is about four miles long and one mile wide.

The Cemeteries

One of the first things the Gaylords did to make their new dwelling place a community apart from New Milford was to set aside land for a cemetery. In the New Milford Town records there is this entry:

> *"January 18, 1737. Then laid out an acre and eight rods of land for a burying place to accommodate our farmers that do or may live near the northwest corner of New Milford Township. It is laid out on the south side of the first small brook south of Aaron Gaylord's dwelling house on the west side of the highway or country road on a round hill near said small brook. Laid out by us.*
> *Stephen Noble and William Gaylord."*

The first graves in the cemetery were those of Mr. and Mrs. Gaylord.

*In memory of Mr. William Gaylord, who departed this
life October the 23rd A. D. 1753 aged 73 years*

The oldest existing records of the cemetery start with February
18, 1863, when a meeting was held in the Village Institute "to take
into consideration the enlarging and fencing of the village burying
ground, and for keeping the same in good condition". The Gaylordsville
Cemetery Association was organized on that date, and a constitution
adopted. Apparently not much was done at that time, as the Association
was reorganized in 1866, and a new constitution drawn up. Orra Warner
was elected President both times, and Orrin Roberts Vice-President.

A committee was appointed to investigate the proposed land purchase. At a later meeting they reported that Mr. Hungerford, who owned the land, wanted $125.00 an acre, all the rails in the old fence, and the use for farming purposes of a carriage path that was to be built on the north side. Also the Association must fence in the whole cemetery and keep the fence in repair. In the event the Association should reject his offer, Mr. Hungerford agreed to leave the matter to two disinterested men provided he could appoint both of them. The land was finally purchased for $85.00 an acre. The new section was up the hill from the old part.

At a meeting in January, 1868, it was voted that any member who had contributed $5.00 or more to the Association would be a member and could select a lot, the highest contributors first, and so on down to the $5.00 ones. Col. H. Merwin was to have the first choice. The remaining lots were assessed and sold later at prices ranging from $10.00 down to $4.00.

After 1870, very few meetings of the Association were held. One was held in 1884, but so few members were present that no business was taken up. The next meeting was in 1891, when a new fence around the cemetery was discussed. In 1892, it was voted to assess all lot owners "to obtain money necessary for the upkeep of the cemetery".

There are no plots left for sale now, although there is an occasional burial there as a member of an old family is placed in the family plot. The cemetery has been endowed by a descendent of the original Gaylords, so its care in the future is assured.

Around 1900 the existing Gaylordsville Cemetery was filling up and there were no longer any plots for sale, so a new piece of ground containing four acres more or less was obtained from Alexander H. Barlow. This cemetery is located a short distance north of the store on the road to South Kent. Here the Morningside Cemetery was created for the purpose of establishing and maintaining a place to bury the dead.

On October 19, 1901, the Morningside Cemetery Association was formed and on November 2, 1901, the original constitution and by-laws were adopted along with a plan for the layout of the cemetery.

The first burial in the cemetery was on December 5, 1901 when Charles Thomas was buried there. In addition to other burials, there were fourteen (14) remains transferred from the Gaylordsville Cemetery in later years and reburied in Morningside along with three (3) from Bulls Bridge Cemetery and one (1) from Kent Cemetery.

There are two (2) Civil war veterans buried in Morningside: Curtis Hall, who died in 1888, and Edmond Hatch who died in 1926. Mr. Hall's remains were transferred from the Gaylordsville Cemetery in 1915.

On December 30, 1976, land containing an additional 0.4 acres more or less was deeded to the cemetery association by Robert and Doris Terhune, with the stipulation that the sale of plots in this section be restricted to residents or former residents of the Gaylordsville Fire District (as such district existed at the date of the deed). These plots are located on the north boundary of the cemetery.

On October 4, 1977, a trust was established at the bequest of Thomas Austin, the first secretary and treasurer of the Morningside Cemetery Association. As stipulated in Mr. Austin's will, this trust is only for the benefit of the Cemetery Association and is to be used for the maintenance and upkeep of the cemetery grounds.

In 1983, stone pillars were erected at the cemetery entrance. These 2 large granite blocks from the old Gaylordsville Bridge pier sat in the middle of the Housatonic River. They were retrieved from the river in 1981 by David and Mary Jane Williamson, using the Gaylordsville Garage wrecker.

In 1977, a large granite sign was erected about 30 feet from South Kent Road and is simply inscribed "Morningside Cemetery."

The Fanton Family Cemetery

There is a third, not so well known cemetery in Gaylordsville, which is located about a quarter mile south of the South Kent town line. It is the Fanton Family Cemetery located on the present Hebert Drive just off of South Kent Road.

THE SCHOOLS

The Gaylord School

By the time the Gaylord settlement was fifteen years old the need began to be felt for a schoolhouse. The children were being taught in the homes, but it was probably felt that it could be done better in a school. In 1740, a schoolhouse was built a short distance south of Aaron Gaylord's house. At first there were only a few families with children in school, and the cost, if any, was divided among them. As the community grew, however, a more businesslike system was needed.

The New Milford records of 1760 show the following entry: "VOTED: that there shall be a district for a school on the west side of the Great River, bounded South by the other district on the west side of said river, west by New Fairfield, east by said river, and to extend north to the north end of New Milford Township." It was later called District 14. This act gave the school committee the authority to set and collect a school tax to meet the costs of maintaining and running the school.

The earliest written records of the school now in existence begin in 1840. Notices of School Committee meetings were posted on the schoolhouse and at the store. Such a meeting was held on August 25, 1840, and the following votes were taken: 1. That James Hungerford be Chairman of the meeting, 2. Warner Marsh, Clerk, 3. Jabez Covill, 1st Comm. and 4. Nathan Gaylord, 2nd Comm., 5. That the Committee shall examine the schoolhouse and have power to make all necessary repairs in and about the schoolhouse in this District, 6. That the price of wood shall be two dollars a cord cut and split suitable for the stove, 7. That two-thirds of the public money be appropriated for the benefit of the winter school, 8. That no scholar residing out of this District shall be allowed the benefit of the public money belonging to this District, 9. That Jabez Covill be collector of school tax, 10. That the meeting be adjourned without date. Vote number six, setting the price of wood, was necessary because the families were allowed to pay a certain amount of the tax in wood for the stove.

The following year William Roberts, Warner Marsh, Joel Bailey and William Knapp were named to the four elected offices. The annual meeting in 1842 ruled that 1/4 cord of wood be allowed for each scholar. In March, 1843, it was voted to have a summer school in addition to the winter school. Though not stated, it appears that the youngest children attended school in the summer, and the older scholars in winter. In September, 1843, the "Inhabitants and Proprietors of District No. 14" were asked to sign a subscription paper to raise "$25.00 for the purpose of erecting a backhouse contiguous to the school." Twelve signers pledged only $11.50.

In 1844, the length of the term was set at four months. It was also voted "that the Canfield children be allowed to attend school in this District if said Canfield teaches the school." In 1848, the Committee was allowed to spend a sum not to exceed $5.00 to repair the siding on the schoolhouse. In 1849, it was voted "that the Committee shall pay not to exceed $1.25 per week for a teacher."

In 1851, a committee of three was appointed to examine the schoolhouse to determine what repairs were necessary. The schoolhouse was then over 100 years old, and lack of money had kept the committee from making any but the most necessary repairs. On October 9, the committee reported that "the schoolhouse will want siding, and the roof will need shingling, together with new seats and a new floor and an addition of one window. Also, said building will want new plastering and painting." The committee also recommended building an addition on the south end of eight feet to be partitioned off for a woodhouse on the west side and an entry on the east side, with a window in the entry. The committee estimated the cost of these repairs to be $200. It was voted to repair the school, but that the report of this committee will be laid upon the table and another committee of three examine the school and see what repairs, additions, and alterations are necessary and proceed to make them by hiring a contractor and binding him with a written contract. A committee was appointed to solicit the inhabitants to raise the money needed.

On October 13, it was voted to "new side the school all over, put in one new window on the west side, put new sash in the windows now in, to relay the floor as needed, remodel and rearrange the seats and desks, and to paint the schoolhouse." The committee was instructed not to build an addition on the south side. On October 16, it was voted to rescind all the votes taken at the October 9th and 13th meetings except the motions to adjourn. It was voted that Nathan Gaylord be a committee of one to "make such repairs as were in his judgment necessary for the present and coming season." In spite of their desires to repair and improve the schoolhouse the committee could not raise the money. Although they had the authority to set a school tax they could not enforce its payment, which was largely up to the conscience of the taxpayer.

Still the committee did not give up. In 1852, a meeting was called to decide whether to repair the school or build a new one. The meeting was adjourned without taking a vote. In 1857, they started again. On September 11, it was voted to move the school one-half of its width and repair it. On September 21, it was voted not to move it there, but to move it onto land west of the highway offered by Ebenezer Sanford for $10.00. On October 7th, it was voted not to move it there, but to move it "so that the west sill of the house shall stand 27' westerly of the center of the house as it is now located and from three to eleven feet southerly." The land could be purchased for $15.00.

Still some were not satisfied. On January 7, 1858, a meeting was held to legalize the building of a new school and out buildings. The cost was to be $455.00, and a tax was laid to collect that amount. However, those who did not favor building a new school refused to pay the tax, and enough money could not be collected. The committee finally decided to abide by the vote of the September 21st meeting. In the summer of 1858, the schoolhouse was moved to the west side of the road and repaired.

With this finally accomplished, matters became fairly routine for a while. Male teachers were paid two-thirds of the tax money or about $160.00. Women teachers were paid about $110.00. In 1872, the schoolhouse was thoroughly repaired and enlarged. Fifteen feet were added to the north end, and the long-talked-of entry and woodhouse were built on the south end. The repairs included a new roof with a cupola, new windows, a new floor, and a new chimney. The original frame, however, remained intact.

After this overhaul, almost no changes were made in the building for many years. The winter term was gradually lengthened, and the summer term finally discontinued. The District School Committee was succeeded by the Town School Board, which later became the Board of Education. Other teachers of that period were Miss Hart, Edith Royce, Miss Tyler, Clifford Marsh, Edith Dean Starr, Agnes Barnum Hum, and Edith Wadhams, though probably not in that order. Next came George Newton, who taught until 1907. He was followed by Charles Soule, who taught until 1915. His place was taken by his daughter, Bessie Soule (Cornwell.) She taught for forty-two years, until 1957. When she retired in that year she had completed a total of fifty years of teaching. During the first half of her teaching in Gaylordsville, very few changes were made in the school building. The heat was still supplied by a coal and wood stove in the center of the room. The only extra light was furnished by four kerosene lamps which were sometimes lit on dark days, but which did little to brighten the room. Going to the nearby homes for a pail of drinking water was a privilege the older boys enjoyed, as it meant ten or fifteen minutes away from their books. Water was used for washing only in emergencies.

In 1895 Miss Jacoby of Falls Village was the teacher.
Shown with her here are the pupils from that time:

Top Row: May Griswold, Lydia Robertson, Agnes Barnum, Edith
Conkrite. Second Row: Anna Mae Morrissey, Clifford Hall, Horace
Hatch, Charles Hall. Third Row: Howard Conkrite, Rena Morrissey,
Genevieve Hungerford (Austin), Loretto Morrissey, Susan Hatch.
Fourth Row: Bessie Soule (Cornwell), Thomas McGoldrick, Angela
Morrissey. Seated: Charles McGoldrick, Phillip Morrissey, and Frank
Morrissey.

This picture was probably taken in 1908, the first
year that Charles Soule was the teacher.

Front Row: Paul Newton, Mabel Roberts, Mamie Hawley, John Malin,
Charles Page, Louis Hungerford, Harold Morey, Harold Hoag, Johnny
Carlson, Madeline Jones, Robert Jones, Vincent Dolan, Theodore
Carlson, John Newton, and Harold Newton.

Back Row: Ronald Disbrow, Mr. Soule, Grace Thompson, Alice Joyce,
Jennie Carlson, Mildred Morey, Bessie Carlson, Mary Newton, Alta
Hall, Elsie Morey, Elsie Carlson, and Florence Hungerford.

A few years late, probably in 1911 or 1912, this picture was taken.

Front Row: Theodore Carlson, William McGoldrick, John Newton, Vincent Dolan, Robert McClaren, Charles Page, Robert Jones, and Harold Newton. Second Row: Bessie Carlson, Veronica McGoldrick, Jennie Carlson, Frank Kaminsky, and Marjorie Roberts. Third Row: Elsie Morey, Paul Newton, Annetta McClaren, Anna Kaminsky, Mildred Morey, and Alta Hall. Back Row: Alice Joyce, Bessie Joyce, Elsie Carlson, and Grace Thompson. The teacher not in the picture was Charles Soule.

Gaylord School 1934

Back row: William Moore, John Flynn, Henry Grisell, Mrs. Cornwell, Betty Cornwell, Helen Hoag and Jane Gibbs. Second row: Jack Moore, Vincent Rosati, Gladys Hills, Mabel Olson, Betty Williamson. Front row: Henry Townsend, Gordon Hills, Charles Dodge, Lucille Grey, Fred Dahl and Edward Donnelly.

In 1935, changes began to take place at the schoolhouse. There were fewer pupils then, and it was felt that it was not practical to keep both the Gaylord and the Waller schools open. The Waller school was closed and all of the students came to the Gaylord school. To help accommodate them in the one school, the seventh and eighth grades were taken to New Milford with the high school students. The old coal and wood stove that had occupied the center of the room for so many years was replaced by an oil heater. Electric lights were installed, and the kerosene lamps discarded.

Bill McGoldrick was a pupil at the red schoolhouse in Gaylordsville from 1937 until 1943. He submitted the following information: "My most vivid memories of life in a one-room schoolhouse always seem to center on wintertime. We often wore our outer coats until late morning when the big pot-bellied stove finally raised the temperature into the '60's. The oldest (or the largest) boy was always in charge of stoking that stove. I remember George Strid held that job for several years. And you could judge how heavily the snow was falling by looking out the west windows to the hemlocks up the cemetery. When you couldn't see them anymore, it was really coming down. And once a week Harold Hunt (the "Music Man") would come up from New Milford to further our musical education. "My Grandfather's Clock" was a favorite of his. Each year he took the new students aside and asked them to sing a scale............ "Do Re Mi, etc." in order to determine their ability to carry a tune. After listening to me he paused for a moment and then said, "Perhaps you could just hum." He was right, of course."

In 1946, the Gaylordsville School Association was formed by the parents, its objective being to improve the general welfare of the Gaylordsville School. One of their first projects was to try to obtain running water in the schoolhouse, but it was not until 1952 that this goal was reached. A well was drilled, and water obtained. A small addition was built on the north end to house lavatories, thus doing away with the outside toilets.

The first meeting of the Gaylordsville School Association was held on November 5, 1946, at the home of Mrs. George Strid. The New Milford Parent-Teachers Association had asked the members of the Gaylordsville group to join them but it was "decided to keep our money here in Gaylordsville," according to information supplied by Alma Edmonds, who was the Treasurer of the School Association the entire time of its existence. Admission fee to each meeting was fifty cents and monthly dues were twenty-five cents. The first officers of the group were: President: Mrs. Al Farnham (Jerry). Vice President: Mrs. George Strid (Josephine). Secretary: Mrs. Frank Piliero (Helene). Treasurer: Mrs. Nelson Edmonds (Alma).

Other members of the group were Mrs. James Hastings, Mrs. Norman Wyble, Mrs. John Cornwell, Mrs. Edward Dolan, Mrs. Stanley Perlowsky, Mrs. Harold Dwy, and Mrs. Jack Dodd. Others joined later when they realized that the school association was a group formed for the benefit of their children. The Gaylordsville School Association served milk and soup at the school, purchased a slide projector and screen, provided film strips and a record player, and put on parties for all holidays, including Halloween and Christmas. The group raised money to purchase playground equipment, sponsored a trip to Danbury, provided games for picnics and helped to get bathrooms installed in the school. Fund raisers included Bingo parties, white elephant sales, College Whist card games, and food and rummage sales, among other things. Money remaining in the treasury when the school closed was used for the purchase of a drop-pendulum schoolhouse clock which is still hanging in the schoolhouse.

Gaylord School 1948 Teacher Mrs. Cornwell

Back row: Judith Piliero, Leo Barto, Lynn Hendrix, Mrs. Cornwell, Jack Sanford, Robert Cornell and Honey Miller. Second row: Raymond Thorland and Harold Cromwell. Front row: Joyce Couchevitz, David Williamson, Stephan Sanford, Frederick (Chip) Farnham, Alan Farnham and Patricia Couchevitz.

As the school enrollment increased the sixth grade and later the fifth grade were transferred to New Milford so only the first four grades were at Gaylordsville. The oil heater was replaced with a hot-air furnace that was installed in the former woodhouse.

In 1957 the four grades were taught by Mrs. Elizabeth Reynolds of New Milford. The students are:

Back row: Susan Cole, Carol Steinman, John Flynn, Harry (Spud) Miller, Linda Ridolfi and Sara Johnson. Second row: Gwen Parker, David Flynn, Deborah Noble, Linda Rebstock, William Bramon and Jennifer Ward. Front row: Kenneth Carlson, Jeanne Taylor, Claudia Gereg and Roxanne Taylor.

In 1961, Mrs. Arthur Newton of Bulls Bridge,
taught three grades at the school.

Back row: John Borniact, Peter Flynn, Lee Hendrix, Dale Parker, Brian Freyenhage, Daniel Primerano, Lee Morsey and Diane Cole. Front row: Russell Chase, Sheryl Beatty, Michael Tuz, June Ridolfi, Carol Chase, Diane Bowler, Lori Flynn and Douglas Terhune.

In 1964, Mrs. Donald Wharton came as teacher of grades one and two, grades three and four having been transferred to New Milford. Early in 1967, the New Milford Board of Education announced that for a variety of reasons they felt that it was no longer practical to keep the school open, and it would be closed in June. Gaylordsville would lose the school where for 227 years its children had started their education. The announcement was received with regret by most of the community. The school, the last one-room school to be operated in the state, had earned their affection during its long career.

The final class in the Gaylord School. The
teacher was Mrs. Donald Wharton.

Front row: Belinda Beatty, Robin Zidack, Karl Fuchs, Jeremy Haase,
John Cox, George Thompson, Barbara Nott and David Peabody. Back
row: Cynthia Eaton, Christine Sanford, Gregory Marsan, Patricia Tuz,
Marie Bowler, Wendy Hendrix, Kim Nott, Diane Pritchard, Race
Meissner, Dawn Irwin and Laura Sheldon.

In 1968, the Town Officials were contemplating the sale of the schoolhouse
since it was longer of any use to the school system. This had always been the
fate of one-room schools no longer used. Two interested residents contacted
Mr. Norris Wildman, the owner of the adjoining property, and discussed the
possibility of preserving the building as an historical site. Mr. Wildman drew
up and circulated a petition to be presented to the town of New Milford.
At a town meeting the same year a resolution was adopted barring the sale
of the building. No deed to the land could be found so it was assumed that
the land would revert to Mr. Wildman. However, in his interest to see the
building preserved, Mr. Wildman agreed to relinquish to the town whatever
rights he might have if the school was to be retained.

The matter of preservation was pursued by contacting the New Milford Historical Society through one of the trustees, and State Senator Alden Ives. Senator Ives went to the State Historical Society to see what funds might be available for this project. The New Milford Historical Society felt the schoolhouse should be kept in the care of the committee from the Village. The rigid requirements of the State Historical Society proved prohibitive. In 1969, after some meetings with the New Milford Board of Finance, a resolution was drawn up and adopted at a town meeting, calling for the restoration and preservation of the school as an historic site. A committee of five persons was appointed by the Board of Selectmen to be in charge of the project, four of them being former students at the school.

The school flag pole is named in honor of Alan Farnham, who died in Vietnam. Mr. Farnham is the only alumnus of the school killed in military service, according to records dating back to World War I. In 1997 the Gaylordsville Historical Society established a scholarship in his memory, which to date has been awarded yearly to a high school senior residing in the Gaylordsville fire district.

In 1998 the school was restored by the New Milford Department of Public Works. They removed the 1960's tile floor and refinished the 100 year-old wooden floor. The plaster work was repaired and painted and the light fixtures polished. Class pictures and school house memorabilia dating back to 1893 are on display.

On July 10th 1999, the Gaylordsville Historical Society hosted a reunion for former students and teachers of the Gaylord School. More than 100 former students and 2 teachers from across the country were among the 275 attendees who enjoyed an old fashion BBQ. Letters were read of schoolhouse memories sent by those who were unable to attend. At the ceremony a new flag was given by the New Milford VFW and the school's old flag was given to Chip (Fred) Farnhan in honor of his brother, Alan Farnham.

At the very successful reunion the following paper entitled "Memorable Moments" was read by Marion Pomeroy Gilbert, who attended the Gaylord School from September, 1936, to June, 1943.

"Having attended the Gaylordsville School for more years than I attended any other educational institution, it is hard to think of just one "memorable moment," so here is a list of some of the things that stand out in my memory:

1. The entry way with its blue and white crockery water jug, later replaced by a modern water bottle inside
2. The teacher's desk with its hand bell that Mrs. Cornwell used to call us in from outside
3. A very stern John Pettibone sitting at that desk once a month to observe us – scary!
4. Graduated desks with the smallest children in front and the "big kids" in back
5. The Pledge Of Allegiance each morning
6. The pot-bellied stove in the middle of the room where Bill McGoldrick toasted his sandwiches in the winter until they were "charbroiled"
7. Doris Chase (Terhune) and I sharing a double desk and being separated for misbehaving and always promising to be good the next time!
8. Going to Mrs. Cornwell's house each afternoon for more water to refill the water jug
9. Recess and lunch time: the brook – Helen Donnelly (Tuz) trying to jump it and usually missing; skating on Silver's pond; the games we played: "Red Rover, Red Rover, let ---come over," "1, 2, 3, Red Light!" and "Fox and Geese" in the wintertime. I remember Anna May Parker (Stolt) running the fence out back and never falling off; the terrible war games where the boys were wounded and the girls patched them up, and of course, the swings and seeing who could pump the highest and jump the farthest off them!
10. The school books…those wonderful oversized geography books about far-away places; boring math books (as I remember) and the "Friendly Village" readers filled with wonderful stories about children who always did fascinating things
11. Mrs. Cornwell reading to us after lunch and many times all afternoon because we usually were able to plead with her to read "just one more chapter"
12. The outhouse where we often lost mittens and hats and anything else that wasn't attached to us!

I have always felt very lucky to have attended a one-room school for seven years. We were happy and carefree and secure, and if we didn't learn something the first time around, we had many more years to get it. Best of all, who can forget the end-of-the-school-year picnics with homemade ice cream and other homemade goodies, and finally the last year at the school, riding home on the tailgate of Norman Wyble's beach wagon – we had arrived!"

The Red Schoolhouse on Gaylord Road continues to be an historical site and meeting place for the Gaylordsville Historical Society. It is open for visitors on Sunday afternoons in July and August and is open the first Saturday in December as part of the "Christmas in Gaylordsville" celebration.

The Waller School

For several years all of the homes in the Gaylord settlement were on the west side of the river. In 1755, however, Ezekial Payne built a house on the east side, about a mile north of the original Gaylord home. Others followed to the east side, and as there was no bridge at that time a school soon became necessary.

This picture of a class at the Waller School
was probably taken in 1884.

Front Row: Charles Talbot, Anna Roche, Susie Hatch, Thomas Austin,
Bessie Austin, Horace Hatch, and Bertha Lampson. Second Row: Ernest
Lampson, Charles Warner, Melville Warner, Lottie Lampson, Moses
Marcy. Third Row: Margaret Honan, Jeanne Honan, Ann Hepburn,
Elvira Austin, Sylvester Hepburn, and Clarence Evans. Fourth Row: Miss
Gregory, Edward Honan, Pauline Roche, Alice Roche. Fifth Row: George
Marcy, Mary Honan, Jack Austin, Lena Hatch and Elizabeth Evans.

An entry in the Town records dated December 16, 1771, reads as
follows: "Voted that there shall be a district for a school beginning at the
northwest corner of New Milford north purchase, thence east by the Kent
line to the south end of Sherman Boardman's farm, thence southward
by the foot of Long Mountain to the south end of Gaylord's field on the
east side of the river, thence by the river to the first mentioned corner and
known by the name of Payne's District." It was District Eleven.

No records have been found to tell when the schoolhouse was built. The oldest record that has been found is a school register for 1867-1868. The teacher that year was Sarah Griffin for the winter term and Cleopatra Sherwood for the summer term. Twenty-nine pupils were listed for the winter term, their ages running from five to seventeen. School opened on October 28, and ended February 14. The pupils had two days off at Thanksgiving and three for New Year's. School was closed on Christmas Day, but they had to make it up the following Saturday.

The summer term began on April 13, and ended September 10. Thirty-four pupils were listed, aged three to thirteen. There were no holidays, but the school was closed one day in June for cleaning. The only member of the school committee listed for that year was James Payne. Unlike the Gaylord School, the Payne District School, or Waller School, as it was later called, was never remodeled or changed, but remained as it was originally built as long as it was used.

This picture was taken in 1896. In the front row is Hattie Brown, Caroline Brown, Lillis, Grisell, Patrick Lillis, Mamie Lillis and Bridget Lillis. Second Row: Robert Dakin, 3 Parsons boys, Ada Brown, Mary Paine, Lena Grisell, Gertrude Grisell, Kilcourse, and Ann Grisell. Back Row: Noel Thomas, Howard Hepburn, George Ward, Louis Talbot, Walter Boinay, Carl Johnson, Howard Conkrite, Miss Smith, May Brown, Marion Underhill, May Parsons, and Melissa Brown.

This picture was taken in 1933. Front Row: Robert Johnson, Thomas Thomas, John Killian, Wilson Parker, Alexander Killian. Second Row: Rosemary Jennings, Edith Thomas, Madeline Wyble, Doris Dwy, Amanda Parker, Mary Ellen Hermanson. Back Row: Pamily Parker, Agatha Mazatta, Richard Thomas, Marguerite Particelli, Florence Pomeroy, William Thomas, Nellie Hine, Irene Wyble, Irving Dwy, Caroline Conkrite, and Robert Dwy.

Two years later, under the watchful eye of Miss Smith, some of the same pupils were there, along with some new ones.

Teachers did not seem to stay long at the Waller School. As one of the former pupils said, "We had a new teacher almost every year". This changed, however, around 1915, when Mrs. Katherine Garvey came as teacher. Mrs. Garvey taught there for 17 years, leaving in June, 1934, to teach at the Boardman School. Elizabeth McMahon taught at the Waller School in 1934 and 1935 and was the last teacher at the Waller District School, as it closed in 1935. The following were students at the Waller School in 1935:

1st Grade: Joseph Killian
2nd Grade: Rosemary Jennings (Beatty)
Edith Thomas (Page)
3rd Grade: John Killian
Virginia Hastings (Smith)

Wilson Parker
4th Grade: None
5th Grade: Alexander Killian
Amanda Parker
6th Grade: Lawrence Parker
Madelyn Wyble
7th Grade: Pamiley Parker (Hills)
8th Grade: Marguerite Partiselli
Agatha Mazatta (Kabetal)
Richard Thomas
Robert Johnson

This information was supplied by Elizabeth McHahon Dolan. She said that the Killian children walked to school from Long Mountain. The names in parenthesis are the married names of the female students, if known.

Right up to the day it closed the schoolhouse remained just as it was originally built. Unlike the Gaylord School, it was never moved, enlarged or remodeled. It never had electric lights or running water. In 1935, it was felt that it was no longer necessary to maintain two schools in Gaylordsville, so over the protests of the parents of the students there, the Waller School was closed, and the children east of the river were transported to the Gaylord School. It was sold, was then used as a summer residence and is now the full-time home of Richard and Maureen Utera, The building still retains its outward appearance as a country school.

Many years after she attended school there, Mrs. John Underhill wrote the following poem about the Waller School,

SCHOOL DAYS

The little schoolhouse under the hill.
Is just as fresh in our memory still
As it was in the days when we went to school
And were taught to live by the golden rule.
The old wooden pail from which we drank
Pure spring water from under the bank
'May I pass the water' was a welcome sound
All drank from one dipper passed around

A map of the world on a wooden ball
Showing the shape of the earth to all
A wooden bench, a little low seat
Where we sat in winter to warm our feet.
Woolen stockings, calf-skin shoes
On our feet in winter we were made to use
Not lace stockings and slippers low
With heels so high we could scarcely go

Under the maple tree, all in a bunch
Huddled together, eating our lunch.
All home made, brought in basket or pail
Fresh made by mother, nothing stale.
Frozen apples, we can taste them yet
Frozen hard, yet easy to get.
Under an apple tree up in the lot
We could go there now to the very spot

A run up the hill where the sorrel grew
Sour as vinegar through and through
We ate with a relish and called it good
We've often wondered how we could
Down to the brook where the waters flow
On to a place called Old Bendago
To slide on the ice, Oh! what fun
Back to the schoolhouse all on a run

No matter how long we're away from home
No matter how far away we roam
Scenes from the schoolhouse under the hill
Will always a place in our memory fill

There were other schools in Gaylordsville that should be mentioned, although very little is known about them. One was a schoolhouse built by Sylvanus Merwin, just north of the Merwinsville Hotel. It was used as a grammar school for the Merwin children and some others, then turned into a girls' specialized school. Some of the girls were local girls; others may have boarded in the hotel.

A girls' boarding school was located in the old hotel that stood on the west side of the river, west of the road just south of the bridge. The girls put out a hand-written newspaper called "The Snowdrop" which contained several essays and a few humorous news items. When the school closed, the hotel was used for apartments.

The Institute was located almost across the road from the Methodist Church. While it was not a high school, it covered some things that were not available in grammar school, such as elocution, public speaking, and current history.

After the Institute was long functioning, the building was sold or given to the Baptists, who had already been holding Sunday services there. The building stood until the 1930's, when it was torn down to make room for a three-car garage.

THE BRIDGES

For nearly seventy-five years when the residents in the Gaylord settlement wished to cross the river, they had to ford it. The usual place was reached by a roadway that left the main road just north of the first Gaylord home. From the west bank, the river was crossed to the lower end of the island that is near the east bank, then up the length of the island and on to shore just above the mouth of the Womenshenuck Brook.

As the village grew on both sides of the stream, the need for a bridge increased. In 1803, the men of the community decided to build one. Native oak and chestnut logs were cut and timbers hewn. Planks were sawed in a nearby mill. The bridge was supported by two wooden piers that stood in the river. The local blacksmith made the bolts and spikes that, along with the wooden dowels, held the structure together.

The site selected for the bridge, picked because the river banks there were higher, was across a stretch of rapids. The swiftly flowing water, especially during flood season and aided by the huge chunks of ice that went down the river in the spring, soon weakened the wooden piers so that by 1815 the bridge was in a very dangerous condition. A paper dated December 12, 1815, reads:

> "Proposal for rebuilding by subscription the bridge across the Ousatonic River, known by the name of Gaylord's Bridge, which to effect we the subscribers whose names are underwritten, do promise we will punctually pay to the Committee appointed to superintend the building of the bridge, in work or timber, the several sums affixed to our names at or before the completion of said bridge".

Sixty-five names were signed for a total of $650.00. This was only about half of the $1,285.00 that was estimated to be the cost of a new bridge. A petition was sent to the town of New Milford asking for a grant of $400.00, but it was refused. The bridge seems to have stood the strain of that winter, as another subscription paper, dated 1816, was circulated. This raised about a hundred dollars less than the first one. Another petition was sent to New Milford asking for $300.00, but it met the same fate as the first one. There are no other records to show whether a new bridge was built or the old one repaired, but whichever it was, the money available must have been aided by a lot of volunteer labor. It then stood the ravages of the stream until 1832, when it again was in a dangerous condition.

Again the community appealed to the Town. The committee in charge of the bridge held a meeting in Peter Gaylord's store on January 16, 1832. They voted to give the bridge to the town, and to present a petition to the town calling for the erection of a new one. The petition was sent in and Selectmen Orrin Bennett, Walter Booth, and John Wooster, issued a call for a special town meeting to be held at the Town House in New Milford on Monday, the sixth day of February. The meeting was adjourned to Monday, March 12, so that the Selectmen could examine the bridge. On that date the following vote was taken: "As it is the opinion of this meeting that it is not expedient to erect free bridges across the Housatonic River, as it affords a facility in crossing to travelers residing out of the town which is seldom, if ever, reciprocated to the citizens of the town when they go abroad; Voted, that provided the bridge about to be erected at the place called Gaylord's Bridge shall be built, either as a toll bridge or as a free bridge, this town will furnish the plank for the first planking of said bridge".

The committee promptly met and rescinded the vote giving the bridge to the Town. They also voted to relinquish all their rights to the bridge to a new company being formed, The Gaylord's Bridge Company, for the purpose of erecting a new bridge, which was to be a toll bridge. A committee was appointed to draw up specifications for the new bridge and decide whether the center pier should be of wood or stone. At a meeting April 5, 1832, William Roberts was elected treasurer of the company, and Warner Marsh, collector. A committee, (Horace Marsh, Daniel Gaylord, and Gerardus Roberts,) was given power to make the contracts for building the bridge and toll house.

The following notice was put up in the store:

> "Whereas the bridge across the Ousatonic River, called Gaylord's Bridge, being in ruinous and dangerous condition, and the public accommodation requiring that said bridge be rebuilt or repaired as soon as possible, the Gaylord's Bridge Toll Bridge Co., Incorporated, agrees to build and maintain a bridge for the convenience and safety of the traveling public. The affairs of said bridge shall be under the direction and government of the stockholders. Toll charges shall be made for all persons, horses or ox-teams passing over said bridge."

Shares of stock were sold for $25.00 a share, and $1,400.00 was raised in this way. Gerardus Roberts submitted a bid to build the bridge for $1,600.00 or $1,800.00. Eight dollars a share was borrowed from the stockholders to bring the cash in their treasury up to that amount. The State Legislature in 1832 granted the Gaylord's Bridge Company a charter allowing them to operate a toll bridge and collect tolls. The bid of Mr. Roberts, of $1,800.00, included building a toll house and taking down the old bridge. There are no records to show how the company fared for the next thirteen years, but evidently not too successfully, for by 1845, the bridge was again in bad condition, and there was no money in the treasury with which to repair it.

On Wednesday, May 21, 1845, a meeting, open to the public, was held at the church, to "take into consideration the condition of the present bridge and to devise means for the speedy erection of a new one." The majority at the meeting favored a free bridge, but would agree to a toll bridge if enough donations could not be obtained to build a free one. A committee was appointed to solicit donations. They were also to take subscriptions for stock in a new Toll Bridge Company, at $10.00 per share, in the event that enough donations could not be obtained. The committee was to report back to a meeting to be held May 31st.

At the May 31st meeting the committee reported that they had been able to get only $356.00 donated for a free bridge, but had been able to get $1,400.00 in subscriptions for stock in a toll bridge. The meeting then recommended that a company be immediately formed to handle the erection and operation of a toll bridge.

The second Gaylord's Bridge Toll Bridge Company was organized on June 17, 1845, under the same charter that had been obtained by the first one. Shares of stock in the old company were exchanged, share for share, for stock in the new one. A committee was appointed to try to sell $3,000.00 worth of stock. The following Board of Directors was elected: William Roberts, Daniel Gaylord, W.B. Ferriss, S.B. Sherwood, and Homer Merwin. A set of by-laws was drawn up and adopted.

At a meeting June 21st, William Roberts and C.S. Gaylord were appointed to examine various bridges in this part of the state, and to determine the best type to be built here. At a meeting a week later they reported on their visits to Boardman's Bridge, Town Bridge, Great Falls Bridge, Zoar Bridge, and a McCauley's Bridge which they considered a poor one. At a meeting July 1st the stockholders decided that an open bridge would serve the company better than a covered one. The Company then advertised for bids for an open bridge 14 feet wide "in the clear."

The bridge was built in 1845 by Warner and Sabins, who also extended the east abutment to give some protection to the tollhouse.

The total cost was $2,812.00. It was supported in the center by a wooden pier, which may have contributed to its short life. For a time the Bridge Company prospered. The 140 stockholders, who held 318 shares of stock received regular dividends twice a year. The main reason for their success was the freight being hauled to Dover, N.Y. The Housatonic Railroad was now completed through Gaylordsville, but the Harlem Valley Line in N.Y. had not yet been built. All freight for Dover came to Gaylordsville and was hauled by team to Dover, using, of course, the toll bridge. A two-horse wagon paid 8 cents for a round trip, a one-horse wagon paid 6 cents. One day's toll, February 6, 1847, totaled $3.02 for the Dover teams. Most of them were hauling for Luther Dutcher, and used the bridge for one-half the regular price. The total tolls for the year amounted to $431.71. The gate-tender's salary was $35.00 a year. Total dividends were $1.60 per share.

Things went fairly well for the Bridge Company until 1854, when disaster stuck again. The spring flood, higher than any remembered before, swept the bridge downstream and demolished it. On May 8, 1854, a meeting was held in the Union church to make plans for rebuilding the bridge. Bids were asked for and the General Assembly petitioned to amend the charter to raise the rates to those of the New Milford Toll Bridge Co., and also to repeal the clause giving free passage to anyone going to or from a gristmill. One of the bids received was from Harris and Briggs. It called for an open bridge 230 feet long, of two spans. Trusses would be fifteen feet high and fifteen feet apart. Vertical trusses would be of cast iron with sway-braces of iron rods. If the Bridge Company furnished the planking, the price would be $10.00 per lineal foot. This bid was apparently not accepted, as the total cost, according to the records, was $2,060.78 1/2. Of this amount, $1,781.00 was borrowed from the stockholders.

The 1854 bridge, showing the toll house at the end. The couple by the bridge may be Mr. & Mrs. Jabez Conkrite, who were the gate tenders for many years.

In 1855, the sides of the bridge were completely closed in to protect the timbers from the weather. In 1857, the wooden pier in the center was replaced by a stone pier built by local men under the direction of Ira Sherwood, who received $2.00 a day, compared to $1.62 1/2 for the other men. Sixty and three-quarter working days were spent building the pier and raising the abutments.

There is some indication that this bridge was converted into a covered bridge as at a stockholders meeting on September 1, 1855, it was voted "that the directors of the Gaylord's Bridge Toll Bridge Company cover the bridge from the bottom to the top stringer, leaving sufficient openings or windows to admit sufficient light."

Again the Toll Bridge Company prospered for a time. Then the Harlem Valley Railroad was built and it was no longer necessary for the merchants of Dover to use the Housatonic Railroad for their freight. The Barlows attempted to keep the Company going by buying up any shares of stock that were offered for sale.

In the spring of 1875 (February), disaster struck again, and the bridge was washed away by an unusually high flood. The bridge at Boardman was also swept away. This time the town of New Milford finally came to the rescue. Agreements were made with all three toll bridge companies, Gaylord's Bridge, Boardman's Bridge, and the New Milford Toll Bridge Company, to purchase their rights and property. New bridges were built at Boardman and Gaylordsville, and all three bridges were free to public travel. The following agreement was made between the Town of New Milford and the Gaylord's Bridge Toll Bridge Company:

> "Know all men by these presents, that the Gaylord's Bridge Toll Bridge Company, a corporation chartered by the State of Connecticut located at New Milford Connecticut, Litchfield County, such directors being by vote of said Company, duly authorized, for the consideration of two hundred and sixty six dollars received to its full satisfaction of the Town of New Milford, do by these presents remiss, release and forever quit-claim unto the said Town of New Milford all right, title, interest claim, and demand whatever which the Gaylord's Bridge Toll Bridge Company has or ought to have in or to the abutments and pier from which said Company's bridge was swept by the ice flood of February last (1875), and whatever rights has or have accrued to the Company by virtue of said act of incorporation, to the bed of the river over which said Company's bridge stood, for the purpose of permitting said Town of New Milford to erect and maintain a free bridge on the site where said Company's bridge formerly stood, and laying out a public highway in the bed and across the Ousatonic at once on its site. Reserving to said Gaylord's Bridge Toll Bridge Company, just compensation (if any) for any damage that may accrue to other property by laying out said highway and building bridges over the same. To have and to hold the premises, with all the appurtenances, unto the said release, its successors and

assigns forever, so that neither the said Bridge Company nor its successors, now any person under it or them shall hereafter have any claim, right, or title in or to the premises or any part thereof, but there from it is and they are by these presents forever barred and secluded, except this above named reservation.

In witness whereof we have set our hands and seals this 26th day of July, A.D. 1875. Signed, sealed and delivered in presents of Robert Kellogg, E.S. Merwin. Gaylord's Bridge Toll Bridge Company, by A.H. Barlow, Joel Bailey, J.M. Pickett, Directors."

Before the new bridge was built the pier and the abutments were built two feet higher to keep the bridge away from the floods. This remained in use for over fifty years, until 1926. Then the State built a new highway through Gaylordsville and a steel bridge was built about one hundred feet upstream.

When the new bridge was completed, the old covered bridge was taken down. The center pier and the abutments remained, though the pier was becoming badly battered by time and floods. During the flood of August 19, 1955, the pier was completely under water for the first time by a depth of about two feet. Eventually the pier all but disappeared.

In 1991 the "new bridge" of 1926 was demolished and replaced by an ugly concrete bridge, much to the dismay of many of Gaylordsville's residents.

PHOEBE BRIDGE ON CEDAR HILL ROAD.

More than likely this bridge was named after Phoebe Gaylord, wife of Daniel Gaylord, who built the house just a hundred yards up the road on the left in 1801. The bridge crosses the Naromiyocknowhusunkatankshunk brook and was the main road into the village until Route 7 was built. Falling into disrepair, the one-lane bridge was closed in 2001 and a new, wider bridge was constructed in its place in 2004.

The Waller Road Bridge crosses the Womenshenuck Brook east of the old Waller schoolhouse. The bridge was rebuilt in 1980 and completely replaced in 1997.

THE STORES OF GAYLORDSVILLE

The first store in the village was in the first Gaylord home. William Gaylord had begun trading with the Indians almost as soon as he arrived in the area, supplying them with seeds and food supplies in exchange for furs. He also taught them the fundamentals of agriculture. As other people settled nearby the business grew. An ell was added on the north side of the house. The door on the left in the picture below was the store entrance. The door on the right of that one was the entrance to a tavern also run by Mr. Gaylord. The family entrance was around on the side of the house. This store was run by Benjamin Gaylord, and later by his grandson, Peter.

Shortly after the bridge was built Peter built a store and a house at the east end of it. The store was completed in 1805 and was run by him for over forty years until he turned it over to his son John.

Peter Gaylord's store became known for miles around. People from all the surrounding country went there to trade and exchange commodities for nearly everything that was wanted. In those days the country merchant was supposed to have or be able to get every article that was wanted. Farmers came there to swap stories and tell each other the news of the day. The porch of the store was provided with benches, and one could find them occupied most any time of the day. Mr. Gaylord was a typical Yankee businessman. The story has been handed down of a woman who brought a pat of butter she had made and asked to trade it for another. It was good butter, she said, but she had found a mouse in the cream when she made it, so she did not want to use it herself. Mr. Gaylord took the butter to the rear of the store, changed the shape of it, and gave it back to her. She went home satisfied that it was not the same butter that she had brought.

While John Gaylord was running the store a shortage of silver money developed. He had some script printed in 1862 to use in place of change. These later came to be called shin plasters.

Following John Gaylord, Charles Gaylord and John Underhill ran the store. A look at the prices of 1880 would make one wonder where there was room for a profit. Pork sold for 11 cents a pound, veal for 9 cents, beef 6 cents, a good steak could be had for 31 cents, a pair of good shoes cost $1.50.

Charles W. Stone was running the store in 1882. He was followed by Henry Disbrow. Mr. Disbrow kept a book for his clerk to refer to. In it he kept a list of all his customers who asked for credit. After each name were character notes and a brief note as to the amount of credit to allow. Such comments as "deadbeat", "lazy, slow to pay" were quite common, as well as "plenty of money", "good for any amount", and one "sell him all he will take".

Following Mr. Disbrow's death in 1901, Edward Honan and Charles Soule bought the store. The partnership was soon dissolved, and Mr. Honan became the sole owner. He ran it for many years, keeping it a true country general store. The stock included not only groceries, but household articles, work clothing, shoes, and even farm implements and supplies. Gradually, with improved transportation and increasing competition from New Milford, some of the lines of general merchandise were dropped to make room for an improved stock of groceries. In 1946, Mr. Honan turned the business over to his son, Thomas, who kept the business in the old building until 1952. By then the old store, nearly 150 years old, was unable to meet the needs of a growing community and increasing trade. A new and larger building was built a hundred yards north of the old one, and the business moved there. Mr. Honan kept the business until 1968, when he sold it to Gerald Nahley. The building was still owned by the Nahleys, while the store had been run by different proprietors. The building has recently been sold, hopefully to continue as a store.

Several years after Peter Gaylord built his store, another store was built on the opposite corner of the South Kent Road by Horace & Warner Marsh. This was also a grocery store, but in addition carried a larger stock of clothing and dry goods than its competitor across the street. The business was later run by Giddings and Barlow, then by Bradley B. Barlow alone. Then by Alanson & William Canfield, followed by Platt and Gaylord, then by John Gaylord alone. Then John Gaylord took over his father, Peter Gaylord's, store and the newer store was run by Pike and Couch; then by Frederick and Edward Starr. Alexander Barlow took over the store in 1859, and ran it until his death in 1912. Mr. Barlow was postmaster from 1869 - 1912, and the post office was located in his store. The building was a double affair, the store using both floors of one section. The ground floor of the other section contained the office of Dr. St. John who practiced there for many years. He was followed by Dr. Couch, Dr. William Graves, and Dr. Barker. The upstairs was occupied by the tailor shop of William Evans, who was in business as early as 1828.

After Mr. Barlow's death in 1912, the store was taken over by Raymond Camp and Philo Gibson. It burned to the ground on April 11, 1915. The fact that with the coming of the automobile a gas pump had been installed in front of the store may have had something to do with the fire, but this was never determined. The property was purchased by George Ward, who erected a two-story building and started selling groceries and meat. He was followed by Jan Pol, who conducted a meat market. Then Frank Barnum put in a full line of groceries, but was unable to compete with the established business next door, and gave up after a year or so. Mr. Pol, who had added living quarters to the rear of the store, returned and started selling second-hand articles and antiques. This building was partially destroyed by fire on November 16, 1969, but was repaired.

The property was purchased by John Flynn and is still owned by the Flynn family.

In 1827, Sylvanus Merwin built a store on the west side of the river, not far from the bridge, and sold groceries and some general merchandise. When the Toll Bridge Company began operating the toll bridge many people on the west side of the river traded at Merwin's to avoid paying the one cent toll charged to walk across the bridge. An additional drawing card was the Jamaica Rum that could be purchased there. Mr. Merwin ran this store until 1843, when he rented this property and moved his operations to buildings he had built next to the railroad right-of-way. He seemed determined to make the railroad the center of town, building a store, hotel, and school along the tracks. The store was run for many years by Mr. Graves, who was related to Mrs. Merwin. It was taken over in 1896 by Edward Honan, who ran it until 1901, when he took over the Gaylord store. Soon after he left, the store at the depot was closed, and the building has completely disappeared.

Agricultural Enterprises

The coming of the railroad brought many changes. The farmers, perhaps, were the most affected. Until that time all their produce, milk, butter, eggs, vegetables, beef, pork, or poultry, had to be peddled about the village, traded at the local stores, or taken to New Milford by horse and wagon. After the railroad came, however, they were able to find other markets, usually in Bridgeport, which was the destination of the southbound trains. Buyers from there would come on the train, make arrangements with the farmers, and give instructions for shipping.

Some of the farmers made extra money selling wood to the railroad, as the engines then were wood burners. A diary of 1850 mentions wood being stacked by the track and also being loaded on cars for Bridgeport. Others sold ties to the railroad. As late as 1905, they were being paid 30 cents apiece for railroad ties. This was not a bad price for those with sawmills, but some sawed them with a two-man cross-cut saw for the same price.

Dairy farming was affected more than anything else. After the contracts with dealers in Bridgeport and other places had been made, the farmers had a market for all the milk they could produce. They brought the milk to the station in ten-gallon cans and waited for the south-bound, or "milk train" to arrive. The cans came back unwashed, on the north-bound, or "can train." The round trip might take two or three days, so several sets of cans had to be kept available. Around 1890 the Willowbrook Dairy, of Bridgeport, built a creamery in Gaylordsville. This was much more convenient for the farmers, as they could bring the milk to the creamery in the morning and not have to wait for the train. Some of the milk was made into butter and cheese, the rest shipped to Bridgeport. Robert Jones was employed by the creamery for many years as a butter maker. Farmers from Sherman also brought their milk to the creamery using a huge wagon pulled by six horses.

The first creamery burned around 1905, and was replaced with a larger one which was operated until 1930. Milk was in much demand, and other companies were sending trucks to pick up the milk. This took so much business away from the creamery that it was no longer practical to keep it open. For a time it was used as a collection point for a truck, but this was given up after a time for a more central location. Some of the trucks would pick up milk right at the farm if a platform was built by the road. After World War II, plagued by high costs and a shortage of farm help, the farmers found it increasingly hard to make ends meet. One by one they went out of business, until by 1973 there were no dairy farms left in Gaylordsville.

Raising tobacco was also quite popular in Gaylordsville. Although most of the tobacco was grown by dairy farmers for a "cash crop", at one time it was called Gaylordsville's million-dollar business. Raising it was a time consuming task, but labor was cheap and most of the farmers raised some. Hotbeds four feet wide and totaling one hundred and fifty feet in length would furnish plants for five acres of tobacco. When the plants were ready to set, three men were needed to work the tobacco setter: a horse-drawn machine that made a furrow, told the men when to set each plant, supplied water, and pulled dirt around the newly set plants. Hoeing had to be done at least twice. When the tobacco was full grown, it was topped to a height of about four feet. This caused the leaves to grow bigger.

It also caused suckers to grow that had to be broken off. A constant lookout had to be kept for tobacco worms that ate holes in the leaves and destroyed their value.

In this area the whole plants were cut and strung on lath and hung in the sheds to cure. In November it was ready to strip and the leaves were picked from the stalks. Storms were anxiously awaited to dampen the leaves so they would not crumble when handled and packed in bundles.

The bundles were taken to the warehouse for sorting and grading. It was not until then that the farmer knew how much he would get for his crop. There were two tobacco warehouses in Gaylordsville. One run by Martin Hungerford, was near the Gaylord School, and a smaller one was on the Morrissey farm. Several men could find winter work in the warehouse. As time went on, higher costs and a shortage of labor, plus the fact that the farmers needed the land to support larger dairy herds, caused them to give up tobacco. The last crop was raised in the late forties.

Another cash crop a few farmers sold was charcoal. Quantities of this were needed by the iron furnace in Bulls Bridge and the lime kiln in Boardman. Usually the company would buy "charcoal rights" and send their own men to cut the trees and do the burning. One of the places this was done was on the Flynn farm where traces of the burning pits can still be found.

Much of the farmers' work was not directly connected with the care of the stock. The winter's supply of wood had to be cut, drawn and sawed. As much as thirty cords or more might be needed to keep the main house and the hired man's house warm all winter. Good planning meant that the wood was cut a year ahead so that it would be seasoned.

Cutting ice was another wintertime job. Some of the farmers depended on cold springs to cool their milk, but most of them did it with ice. When the ice on the ponds or river was thick enough, from twelve to eighteen inches, it was sawed out in cakes, sometimes two feet square. These were stored in the ice house and covered with sawdust. This would keep it all summer to cool the milk and supply the ice box in the farmhouse pantry. The creamery also needed large quantities of ice to keep the milk cool on its journey to Bridgeport. A large ice house was built adjoining the creamery. At ice cutting time the farmers were hired to haul the ice from Creamery Pond, being paid so much a load. The story had been told of one man who fell in the pond while loading his sled. Instead of going home for dry clothes, and so missing a few loads, he ran beside the sled for the rest of the day to keep from freezing. There was also a small ice house behind the store to supply ice to keep the butter and meat cool.

In the summer some time had to be spent raising potatoes for the year's supply. A good potato cellar was a real asset to keep the potatoes in good condition until the following summer. Most farmers raised enough so that some could be sold in the village or traded at the store. Corn had to be raised to be fed to the horses or ground into dairy feed at the grist-mill. The corn was cut and stacked in the fall, when the ears were ripe. Later in the fall or early winter, the ears were picked and husked, and the stalks cut up for the cows. When silos came into use, more corn was raised and cut green to be chopped and stored in the silo to be fed to the cows all winter, or as long as it lasted.

Haying also took a lot of the farmer's time. Before the hay baler came into use the loose hay was drawn into the barn and stored in the mow. A load of hay being drawn by a good team of horses made a nice picture, but it represented a lot of hot, dusty work.

1894 Newton Farm, one of the last remaining farms in Gaylordsville. Originally owned by the Newton family, the farm has transitioned from dairy to beef and is now owned by the Lescynski family.

The Blacksmith Shop was an important place. At one time there were several in the village. Some of them were near wagon shops, and the blacksmiths spent more time making nails, bolts and hardware for the new wagons and carriages than they did shoeing horses. One shop of this sort was on the farm now owned by the McGoldrick's. Another was near Mill Pond, on the Mud Pond Road, where there was a wagon shop that specialized in heavy wagons used to haul iron ore from the South Kent mines on Ore Hill.

Another shop, that may have been one of the first, was on the west side of the river just south of the bridge. When not shoeing horses, the blacksmith there made flatirons. This shop was destroyed when the dam burst in 1854. A new one was built on the top of the bank almost opposite the Church. The building still stands, unused except for storage.

Still another blacksmith shop stood just east of Liberty Hill. Very little is known about it except that William Jennings, who later took over Brown's Forge, learned the trade there. In addition to the farm and carriage horses of the area, some of the horses that hauled the iron ore from South Kent to the furnaces in Bulls Bridge and Kent were brought to Gaylordsville to be shod. During the peak of this activity a new shop was built that remained in business long after all of the others had closed. In 1870 Amos Brown built a new shop west of the railroad, about a half mile north of the station for his two sons, Homer and Henry. They had already learned the trade in a shop about a quarter mile north of the new one, on Long Mt. Road. Mr. Brown installed a forge and anvil for each son. In 1871 they opened the shop, calling it Brown's Forge, the name it still has.

Brown's Forge

Homer Brown died in 1899 when he was only 42 years old. Henry carried on in the business alone until 1913 when William Jennings, Homer's son-in-law, joined him. Henry died in 1926, and Mr. Jennings continued running the shop until his death in 1942.

It was last run by Nathaniel (Nat) Ashman who did more wood-working, axe handles and other things, than he did horse shoeing. It finally closed its doors in 1962.

Harriet Sebelia Brown (Hattie) was born on March 11, 1893, daughter of Esther Thorp Brown and Homer Brown (one of the Brown's Forge Browns.) Hattie married Frank Odlum in 1916. Mr. Odlum was the Station Agent at the Merwinsville Hotel for a few years, and at the time of his death in 1920 was the station agent in Stockbridge, Massachusetts. Hattie then married James Anderson in 1932. He died in 1968.

THE OLD BROWN HOUSE

Pictured are: Henry Amos, Camila Homer (holding May), Caroline Sheldon Brown, and Esther. The building was torn down in 2011.

Hattie lived in the family home on Brown's Forge road, right next to the old Brown house. This home was built in 1893.

Hattie was a bright, energetic little lady who loved to have visitors and always enjoyed talking about the forge and her memories of Gaylordsville. In 1970, Mrs. Hattie (Brown) Anderson deeded the land and building to the New Milford Historical Society so it could be preserved as an historic site. Hattie passed away on September 25,1990.

After a few years the Gaylordsville Historical Society was formed. Brown's Forge was then deeded to the Gaylordsville Historical Society in 1997 and the GHS has done extensive work to preserve this historical forge. Following the acquisition of the building, it was open for many years on Sundays in the summer, hosted by Alan Dodd, Jack Dodd, and Jimmy Dolan. It continues to be open on Sundays in July and August, hosted by volunteers.

Among more recent memories, the late Maybelle Jennings Thomas recalled handing nails and tools to her father, William Jennings, when he shod horses. She said that when she was older and her father started going to farms to shoe horses, she would drive him. Both Alan Dodd and Maybelle Thomas recalled farmers would stop with their teams of work horses on their way back from the local creamery to have them shod or to have their wagons repaired. The mean horses had to be put in a wooden frame in order to be shod. This structure can still be seen at Brown's Forge, along with the original tools used for the shoeing.

Another business that thrived for many years was known as the lumberyard, although lumber was not always the main item sold. The business was started before 1880 by Levi Stone and Charles C. Pomeroy. They dealt mainly in working oxen that they brought in on the railroad from Massachusetts, a carload at a time. They were already trained for work, and were sold to farmers from a wide area.

In 1880 Eric Helsten joined Mr. Pomeroy, and they expanded the lumber business, building some new sheds and keeping a larger supply on hand. This also was brought in on the railroad, both northern and western lumber being kept in stock. Mr. Pomeroy's son, Henry, took over the oxen, and also sold horses as farmers began using them more in place of the slower oxen.

Around 1900 farm machinery was added to the business. This proved to be such a successful venture that the selling of oxen and horses was eventually given up. Paint, farm tools and building hardware were also sold. The business was gradually turned over to Henry's son, Charles. In later years the farm machinery business was run separately as the Housatonic Tractor Company and was eventually moved to New Milford by Mr. Pomeroy's son-in-law. The lumber business was continued by Mr. Pomeroy until his death in 1964. The buildings were purchased by Aaron Seltzer and used as a private residence up to the present time.

INDUSTRIES

In 1807, a dam was built across the river a short distance north of the bridge. It appears to have been built by a John Wilkinson. Peter Gaylord purchased a one-third interest in the dam from Mr. Wilkinson for $700.00, according to a deed of 1813. Mr. Gaylord built a gristmill on the east bank of the river. This mill had several sets of stones so that several lots of grain could be ground at the same time, either for cattle feed or into flour and corn meal. A house for the miller was built nearby, and was occupied for many years after the mill was gone.

On the west side of the river, taking its power from the same dam, was a woolen mill, with all of the necessary machinery for taking the raw wool from the farms and making cloth. Machinery was also added to make satinet, an imitation satin. Just above the woolen mill was a saw mill and shingle mill, on the second floor of which was a factory where hubs, spokes and other wagon parts were made. Another product was a patented grapple used by fishermen. They also made mattresses filled with the shavings from the shop. The principal owner of both of these mills was William Roberts, whose enterprise brought Gaylordsville much of its prosperity. He bought pine logs in Canaan, and during the high water in the spring these would be rafted down the river to his mill.

South of the woolen mill was a blacksmith shop and knife factory. Knives bearing the mark of "Marsh and Taylor," or "Taylor and Company" were made. Below the blacksmith shop was a tannery run by Merritt Platt. This was later converted into a wagon shop run by Bennett Monroe. The knife factory, tannery and woolen mill got their power from the dam by means of a canal that went under the road near the west end of the bridge.

Mr. Roberts also started a marble quarry on the east side of the river a short distance north of the dam where a fair grade of marble could be found. When the Housatonic Railroad reached Gaylordsville, he started work on a connecting railway to run to his quarry. Some work had been done on the roadbed when he decided to sell all of his businesses to Charles Stearns and Josiah Sturges of Brooklyn N.Y., which he did in 1850 or 1851. The new owners planned to finish the railway spur, and reached an agreement with Morris Barnes, through whose land it would pass. Mr. Barnes had a grist mill and plaster mill on the Womenshenuck Brook and was very particular in the agreement concerning bridges, culverts and cattle passes. He also reserved the right to construct a branch line to his mill. However, although some additional work was done on the roadbed, no tracks were ever laid. Mr. Barnes later sold his mill to Bradley Barlow, who added a cider mill. Near the gristmill and getting its water power from the same dam on the Womenshenuck, was the foundry of William Talbot. The plows, tools and other farm implements made there were famous for their quality.

The sawmill and woodworking shop upstream from the dam

West of the Roberts woodworking mill, on the Wimisink Brook where it joins the river, was another tannery. This was run for many years by Eric Helsten. Mr. Helsten rebuilt a dam on the Wimisink a few rods west of the tannery and ran a grist mill there. This mill was unique in that the water wheel was under the mill instead of on the outside. The wheel was later replaced by a horizontal, steel turbine with a vertical shaft. This turned the mill wheels faster with a smaller amount of water. The mill was then being run by Charles Evans, and was last run by Bert Booth. It went out of business in the late 1920's.

In 1854, tragedy struck many of the Gaylordsville industries. Spring floods caused the river to rise, according to one account, twenty-three feet. The Gaylord grist mill, the woolen mill, the woodworking mill, the tannery and the knife factory and the dam itself were all swept away, most of them never to be replaced. John Taylor built a new blacksmith shop up on the bank nearer the road and Bennett Monroe built a new carriage shop east of the river on the hill behind the Monroe house. The rest of the buildings were not replaced and Gaylordsville's future as an industrial community was suddenly ended.

There were several small mills of various types located around the village. In the early days considerable flax was raised in the area to supply fibers for the homespun cloth used by many housewives who made garments and other articles from it. On the bank of the Wimisink Brook a short distance west of the village, was a mill for breaking the fibers and hetcheling the flax, preparing it for spinning and weaving. The mill was owned by John Seeley, and in it he met a tragic death, being crushed in its machinery. South of the village, on the Naromiyocknowhusunkatankshunk Brook, was another mill supported by the flax growers. Here the flax seed was ground and linseed oil produced. The bridge just north of the Morrissey farm is still occasionally referred to as Old Mill Bridge. Further up the brook was a saw mill that also made wagon parts. Nearby was a blacksmith shop that devoted much of its time to making nails and bolts. Also, somewhere in that area, was a kiln where bricks were made from native clay. Still farther up the brook was a cider mill. Buttons were made in at least two locations, one near the Gaylord school, and one in Squash Hollow. Henry Piercy ran a harness making shop on what is now the Carlson farm, in the same building previously used by Roger Sherman for his shoemaking. Near the north end of the village, on the Mud Pond Road and on the brook coming from Mud Pond which was dammed at that point to form Saw Mill Pond, was a saw mill, grist mill, wagon shop and blacksmith shop. The saw mill stayed in business the longest and was last run by the Thomas family, still using the old "up and down" saw.

About three miles south of Gaylordsville was Buck's Mill. This mill had what may have been the biggest water wheel in the area. An overshot wheel, it got its water by means of a trough over three hundred feet long. The inside of the wheel was lined with metal gear teeth that meshed with a gear on the mill shaft and turned it at high speed with the power developed by the huge wheel. Inside the mill the power was distributed by an elaborate system of shafts, pulleys, and belts, to run a saw mill, cider mill, and machine shop for both wood and metal working. The mill was run until around 1953, the power then being furnished by a gasoline engine.

Buck's Mill

The last mill to begin operations and the one that was the last to go out of business was the mill on the Flynn farm. Unlike most of the other mills in the area that were run by water power, this one was run by a large stationary steam engine that had been purchased from the hat shop on West Street, New Milford, when it closed in 1891. Business began there in 1892 with a grist mill. Later a threshing machine and fanning mill that had been run by horsepower were run by the steam engine by means of a three hundred foot rope belt. Next a saw mill and shingle mill were added.

The engine was also used for such farm chores as filling silos and sawing wood. A wood lathe was also turned by it, and even a grindstone. When in use, the engine gave off clouds of steam which passers-by who were unaware of its presence would mistake for smoke and would dash to the house to report that the barn was on fire. The grist mill was last run in 1938. The saw mill was used occasionally until 1965, when it too, became silent.

BUSINESSES

As in all parts of the country, the old roads in Gaylordsville were unable to cope with the growing popularity of the automobile. The road from New Milford to Gaylordsville on the west side of the Housatonic was no exception. For this reason most people in the area were pleased to learn that a federal highway, U.S. Route 7, was to follow this path.

Work on the road started in the early twenties. As it wound its way towards Gaylordsville, it followed the old road until it was about a mile south of the village. There, instead of going over Cedar Hill, the concrete highway kept to the east, cutting through former tobacco fields and farm land, rejoining the old road as it reached the edge of the village. The covered bridge was not adequate for the new road, and a steel bridge was built about a hundred feet up stream. The road continued north, winding past the power house with sharp curves.

New business places soon appeared along the new road. Where the new and the old roads joined south of the village, Emanuel Williamson opened the Gaylordsville Garage in a converted cow barn in 1923. The garage soon became a favorite gathering place for the men of the village, whether their cars needed repairing or not. Many car owners learned more about their cars there than they could from the car owner's guide. The garage continued doing business at the same location for many years. After Manuel's death in 1973, the garage was taken over by his son, David and his wife, Mary Jane, who were the proprietors for many years, retiring in 1990.

Half a mile south of the garage, Mr. and Mrs. Way opened the Red Rose Arbor in 1926. Specializing in hot dogs, ice cream, candy and soda, it soon became very popular with children and grown-ups alike. Mr. Way opened a gas station across the road. Mr. and Mrs. Louis Collins built a group of overnight cabins nearby, called the Tom Thumb Cabins. For several years they were the only ones for miles in either direction and were filled nearly every night all summer. The three businesses prospered for many years until Mr. and Mrs. Way retired and moved to Florida.

Also in 1926, George Ward built the Basket Shop just north of the new bridge. Hand-woven baskets, pottery, gifts and souvenirs were available to attract the tourists. Mr. and Mrs. Ward ran the shop for over twenty years, then sold it to Alonzo (Al) S. Farnham. Mr. Farnham also kept it for almost twenty years, during which he added a nursery and garden shop. Mr. and Mrs. DeWolfe Hotchkiss bought it in 1967, and now son, Reed Hotchkiss is the proprietor!

Over the years several doctors have practiced in Gaylordsville. The earliest records show Dr. Gamaliel St. John to be the village doctor from 1830 to 1850, having an office next to Barlow's store. His income was evidently not very high, as he supplemented it by acting as toll collector at the bridge which was right across the road from his office. Dr. William Graves was here for a while, as was Dr. Charles Couch, who was practicing here in 1867. Dr. Baker was mentioned in a diary of 1896 as having set a broken leg for ten dollars.

Dr. Dolan, wife, and passengers Henry Pomeroy and wife

Dr. John Dolan was probably here longer than any of the others, maintaining an office from 1866 to 1912. The last one to live and practice here was Dr. Henry Turrill. He used some of his spare time organizing and leading a Boy Scout Troop until he moved to Kent in 1918.

Dr. Mortimer Northrup was a dentist, and lived a short distance south of the church in the late 1800's. He also felt the need to supplement his income and raised vegetables to sell. He probably did not make much money this way either, as the signs read: "green peppers 10 cents a dozen; grapes 5 cents a bunch; tomatoes 3 cents a quart."

Daniel Gaylord was a professional photographer who had a studio over Gaylord's Store in 1848. He used a Daguerrotype camera, and occasionally opened temporary studios in other communities. Several years later the same rooms over the store were being used by a barber.

William K. Evans was a tailor, and had a shop upstairs next to Barlow's Store from 1828 to 1849. He would make a coat for $3.50, or pants for $2.50. A vest cost only 75 cents. He would also cut out garments, and the housewife could take the pieces home and do the sewing herself. The shop was later run by M.A. Kidd, who was in business in 1870.

Several shoemakers have plied their trade here, among them Roger Sherman, who lived here from 1846 to 1848. According to legend Mr. Sherman thought his house was in the town of New Milford, when actually being just north of the Wimisink Brook it was in the town of New Fairfield, which then included all of the present town of Sherman. Mr. Sherman was quite surprised when he received a tax bill from New Fairfield, and refused to pay it. He soon moved to New Milford and it is not known whether he paid the taxes or not. Over one hundred years later the same shop was used by Henry Piercy for harness making.

THE GAYLORDSVILLE VOLUNTEER FIRE DEPARTMENT

The people of Gaylordsville had long felt the need for better fire protection. The New Milford firemen were too far away to give good protection to this community. During the few years preceding World War II there were several fires in the village that had disastrous results. The first house built here, in later years known as the Hall house, burned to the ground in 1940. It was a small fire when it was discovered and could have been easily extinguished had a fire truck been available, but by the time one arrived from New Milford, the fire had spread rapidly through the old house and was beyond control.

This and other similar events emphasized the need for a local fire department. After the war several people in the community decided it was time to do something. Several public meetings were held during which it was decided that the best way to approach the problem would be to organize a volunteer fire department. On October 21, 1946, fifty-five men signed up as being willing to join. The following men were charter members of the Gaylordsville Volunteer Fire Department;

Henry Grisell, Edward Dolan, Charles Jones, Charles Pomeroy, Alan Dodd, Norman Wyble, Harold Newton, Albert Miller, Richard Gebhardt, Thomas Dodd, Harry Furnside, Frank Piliero, Henry Rydell, George Lawson, James Hastings, John Malin, George A. Strid, George Karcher, John Barton, Arch Sanford, Lowell Hendrix, Frederick Dahl, George Strid, Jr., Edward Goldspink, John Flynn, Theodore Carlson, Leroy Booth, Frank Beach, A.E. Williamson, Arthur Ball, Thomas Honan, William Dike, John Magyar, Wesley Pomeroy, James Dolan, Harold Dwy, George Ward, Clarence Hendrix, Al Farnham, Vincent Rosati, John Cornwall, Kenneth Post, Leo Rosati, Albert Trautman, Richard Bellemare, William Leviness, Steve Gereg, Edward Noble, Wilson Parker, Thomas Austin, Martin Tomasovski, Theodore Booth, William McGoldrick, Alan Parker and Chris Thorland.

On October 28th the first meeting of the new company was held, and the following officers elected: Chief, Harry Furnside; Captain, Charles Jones; First Engineer, Henry Grisell; Second Engineer, Leroy Booth; First Lieutenant, Emanuel Williamson; Second Lieutenant, James Hastings; Treasurer, Richard Gebhardt; Financial Secretary, Alan Dodd; Secretary, John Flynn. Board of Directors: Frank Beach, Thomas Honan, Arthur Ball, Albert Miller, and Charles Pomeroy. The new Chief had been a member of the Schenectady, New York, fire department and was instrumental in getting the new department properly organized. Also a great help was Louis Maas, an ex-chief of the Bayshore, Long Island, N.Y. Fire Department.

Committees were appointed to draw up a Constitution and By-laws, start fund-raising activities, and to look for equipment. Meetings were held every week in the Grange Hall. A demonstration was held in Jones' field, testing the time it took two types of trucks to put out similar fires. Two shanties had been built and were set afire at the proper time. The climax came when one of the shanties blew up, but the demonstration was a success. With the help of Mr. Maas, the first truck was purchased from the Bayshore Fire Department - a 1921 American LaFrance, which was obtained for $260. The second truck was discovered by Chief Furnside in the Schenectady Army Surplus Depot, a 1942 Army-type Chevrolet; it had never been used and was available for $800. Although some of the men questioned the need for two trucks, it was felt that this was too good a bargain to turn down. Only the LaFrance was put into service the first winter, as the Chevy had to be cleaned up and painted. These two trucks comprised the Department's equipment for ten years, and the Chevrolet is still in use as a parade vehicle.

The next big problem was a firehouse and where to put it. The trucks were housed in private buildings the first year while several sites were considered. Finally a site on Route 7 at the east end of the bridge offered by Mr. And Mrs. Clarence Evans was accepted. The Finance Committee had been canvassing the community, and the Department had been holding some fund-raising events. In July, 1947, they held their first carnival, making a profit of about $1500. Although they had only about half enough to close in a fire house they felt that it should be done rather than try to get through another winter the way they had the previous one.

In September, work on the building was started. Most of the work was done by the firemen so that what money they had could be used for materials. In November the two-bay firehouse was completed enough so that the trucks could be kept in it. No work was done on the meeting room upstairs at that time. The winter that followed was a hard one financially. The bank balance shrank to less than two hundred dollars, while over one thousand dollars of the building debt remained. That summer, however, another successful carnival made it possible to pay their debts. That fall the outside of the firehouse was completed, but it was another four years, in 1952, before the meeting room upstairs was finished. On October 18, the sixth anniversary supper was held in the newly finished room.

Until 1952, the fire district limit had been two miles, but in that year it was extended to three miles, giving many more families the benefit of quicker response to calls, in addition to lower insurance premiums. Also in that year fire call telephones were installed in three locations, with alarm buttons to make it easier to turn in an alarm. In 1956 the firemen decided that the 1921 LaFrance was no longer suitable for good fire protection. It was replaced with a 1956 Ford that was delivered in April. The LaFrance was sold to the Robertson Bleachery in New Milford.

In 1957, it was learned that the ball field, where the firemen's carnivals were held, was up for sale. In order to preserve it both as a ball field for the community and as a place for their carnivals, the Department bought it and several years later purchased the Hall property north of it. In 1959, to continue the steady improvement in equipment and service, two-way radios were installed in both trucks, and three years later a base radio was installed in the firehouse.

1965 saw the organizing of the Ladies' Auxiliary to help the firemen in their fund-raising projects, bring coffee and sandwiches when the men were on duty for long periods, and to help in many other ways. They purchased a resuscitator for the Department that has proved to be useful many times. It is important to note that the Ladies also played a key and pivotal role in the early days of the Fire Department. Since the Fire Department could not afford to have an answering service handle the fire calls, three telephone numbers were listed and were to be called in case of fire: the Farnham, Beach and Dodd households. Siren switches were installed at the homes of these members. The system worked well and the women did a good job of making sure someone was always there to answer any fire calls. In case one might fall or be injured in the hurry of getting up in the middle of the night to answer the phone and blow the siren, they were made members of the Fire Department so they were covered by the department's insurance. Gaylordsville was one of the first Fire Departments to have women members.

The following women were charter members of the Gaylordsville Volunteer Fire Department Ladies Auxiliary: Caroline Chase, Salome Neelands, Vivian Cornell, Emily Parker, Susan Fredlund, Josephine Pol, Bertha Gereg, Martha Sanford, Charlotte Hendrix, Jean Sheldon, Ruth Larson, Barbara Thorland, and Mimi Burkhardt.

The area near the ball field had always been a difficult place to get water quickly. To remedy this, in 1966 a reservoir was installed underground on the north end of the former Hall property and a hydrant put on it. Ironically, it is almost on the site of the house that burned for lack of a quick water supply.

About this time the firemen began to look ahead to the time they would be getting another truck. As they had decided that it would be in addition to the two present trucks, not a replacement, the firehouse would have to be enlarged. Plans were drawn up, and in 1967 an addition was started across one end and all the way across the back of the original building. This would provide space for three more vehicles. Also, in 1967, a memorial donation that had been given in memory of Mr. Frank Beach was used to drill an artesian well on the firehouse property. This permitted the abandoning of a fifty-year-old pipe line to a nearby spring that had been giving dubious service for a number of years.

In November, 1968, a committee was appointed to investigate new fire trucks and bring in a recommendation in February, 1970, as to what type of truck the department should buy, and its specifications. In 1969, the department was given a used tank truck by the Alfred Lane family. It was repaired and painted by the firemen, and made a valuable addition to the department's equipment. In February, 1970, the new truck committee gave their report. They recommended the purchase of a Ford pumper-tanker at a cost of $29,000. The members agreed, and the truck was ordered. It was delivered in September, 1971. It gave the firemen a lot of satisfaction to be able to pay cash for it. The Fire Department's equipment after twenty-five years of existence consisted of four trucks housed in a spacious firehouse, all paid for through the efforts of the firemen, with cooperation of the residents. On their 25th anniversary, twenty-four firemen received pins in recognition of twenty-five years of service to the community.

The department expanded further in 1990 with the building of a stand-alone 4 bay addition which was needed to house new apparatus. As of this writing the fire department is celebrating its 70th year of service to the Gaylordsville community. A minor renovation to the original firehouse is in the planning stages and the department currently has nine pieces of apparatus.

In 1996 a fiftieth anniversary parade was held with firemen and apparatus from many surrounding towns participating in the festivities.

Over the years many Gaylordsville residents have given their time and energy to the fire department in order to provide a safe environment for the community. The men listed below are those who have served the department in the role of Chief:

Harry Furnside, Al Farnham, Charles Jones, Ed Dolan, Alan Dodd, Elmer Carlson, Thomas J. Dodd, Robert Johnson, Howard Sheldon, Lowell Hendrix, Edwin Larson, Allen Parker, Howard Fredlund, Steven Sanford, Nelson Edmonds, Jr., John Flynn, Jr., Phil Jejer, Lee Hendrix, A. Jeff Parker, Jon Jejer, Paul Loormann, Wendell Peters, Mike Pryor, Steven Pryor, Tom Hogan, Karl Fuchs, and David E. Williamson.

In 2003 the Gaylordsville Volunteer Fire Department launched their web page on the Internet, www.gvfd.com, where current statistics and information concerning the department can be found.

THE CHURCHES OF GAYLORDSVILLE

Until 1824 no regular religious services were held in Gaylordsville. Traveling preachers occasionally held services in the schoolhouse, but usually those wishing to attend church had to make the seven- mile trip to New Milford. In 1824 Rev. Cyress Silliman of the New York Conference, came to visit his cousin, Mrs. David Sterling, on Stilson Hill. While he was visiting there Rev. Silliman held meetings four evenings in the Gaylord School. The result of those meetings was a class of nineteen Methodists and another of twenty-six Congregationalists. Eighteen of those forming the Methodist Church were Benjamin B. Soule, Homer Waller, Martha Waller, Peter Gaylord, Elizabeth Gaylord, Truman Gaylord, John Gaylord, Laura Hendrix, Polly Pine, Clarissa Judd, Sally Judd, William Terry, James A. Hungerford, Spencer Ward, Herman Stone, Rufus Burman, and David Jones.

Subscription papers were soon circulated to raise money to build a meeting house and in 1825 a Union church building was built near the store on the east side of the river. It was used alternately by the Methodists and the Congregationalists and a few years later by the Baptists, who had then organized a Church Society. Rev. Aaron Hunt preached the first sermon in the new church. There is almost no information available on the activities of the Congregational Church. The Methodist Circuit at that time was made up of these preaching places: Pleasant Plains, Brookfield Iron Works, Newtown, Hawleyville, Northville, Merryall, Kent Mountain, Bulls Bridge, Long Mountain and Gaylordsville. There were only three churches on the circuit. At the other places services were held in schoolhouses or private homes.

The circuit rider was always welcome at the homes of Methodist families in the community, and it was considered a privilege to entertain him. The dates that some of the earliest circuit riders served are not known, but their names are as follows: John Reynolds, William Jewett, Fitch Reed, Samuel Cochran, Seth Scofield, Uriah Fisher, Charles Steane, William H. Barnes, Benjamin Bedford, Frederick Brown, Joseph Hinson, Aaron Hill, and Francis Donnelley.

In 1837, Merwin Richardson served the circuit, and in 1838 Alonso Selleck. The Methodists on Long Mountain soon decided to join with the Gaylordsville Church and a little later in 1844 or 1845, during the pastorate of Gad S. Gilbert, the Kent Mountain and Bulls Bridge groups also joined the Gaylordsville Church. Some services were still held in each locality, presumably on the Sundays the Congregationalists or the Baptists were using the Union Church. In the oldest record book of the Church now in existence, a minister had written some notes for his successor, telling where he could count on being invited to dinner or supper, and where he would be welcome to spend the night after an evening service.

In 1846-1847 Elias Gilbert was the pastor; 1848-1849, Justin O. Worth; 1850, Thomas Treadwell; 1851, William Wake; 1852, Alexander McAllister. Both the Methodists and the Congregationalists were feeling the desire for a church of their own, and in 1853, during the pastorate of Gilbert Hubbell, subscriptions were taken by both societies to raise the necessary money. The Methodists' drive was successful, and in 1854, during the pastorate of David Nash, the present church was built. The land was given by Rev. John Gaylord, who also was in charge of the subscription drive that raised $2800 toward the cost of the new church.

The Congregationalists' drive did not succeed, and after due consideration they decided to disband, many of them becoming Methodists. The Trustees of the Union Church building offered to give it to the Baptists, if they would keep it in repair and use it for their services. The Baptists, being a small group, felt that it was too large for their needs and did not accept the offer. It was later sold to Peter Gaylord, who moved it a short distance and converted it into a barn. It was moved again in 1925 to make room for the state highway, and has since been taken down.

The Gaylordsville Church was now in the New York East Conference, as the New York Conference was divided in 1848, placing this church in the Eastern division. Rev. Nash remained as pastor until 1855; 1856-1857, William Stebbins; 1858-1859, Thomas Littlewood; 1860-1862, John H. Gaylord; 1862, William Ross; 1864, John H. Gaylord. It was during Rev. Gaylord's second stay, in 1864, that the Church sheds were built. They provided shelter for the horses and carriages and later the autos, of the church-goers. They were torn down around 1950 to enlarge the parking area.

In 1865, Rev. Benjamin Gelman became the second minister to marry a Gaylordsville girl when he married Fanny Turkington. Rev. Hubbel, who married Frances Graves was the first; 1867-1868, F.W. Lookwood; 1869-1870, Sherman Barnes. The oldest existing church record book of this church begins with 1871, when Frank Jordan was pastor. The first entry reads: "Church Record for the Methodist Episcopal Church, Gaylordsville. Arranged in alphabetical order and classified by the Circuit for the year of our Lord 1871. Being revised from the old Records as left by Sherman D. Barnes, deceased, the last pastor of this Circuit. Frank F. Jordan, Pastor, 1871."

Another entry in the old Record reads: "The General Conference of 1872 attached Gaylordsville to the New York Conference, which was subsequently supplied by B.M. Genung, who had been appointed to South Dover, N.Y. Bulls Bridge was included in the transfer with Gaylordsville. B.M. Genung."

Rev. Genung lived in the parsonage in South Dover (Wingdale) and preached in Gaylordsville Sunday afternoon. This plan was followed only two years. In 1874-1875, Uriah Symonds served as pastor, and lived in the rooms over the store. In 1876, Rev. W.A. Dalton came and lived in a house near the lumberyard.

In 1876, Mrs. James Paine was appointed as the first Sabbath School Committee, as the Sunday School Superintendent was then called. The Sunday School has been operated continuously since then and has been an important part of the church. In 1877-1879, Robert Elsden was pastor, and during his stay the first parsonage was purchased from Wesley Ward. It was the first house on the left on the Evans Hill Road. Many years later it burned, and the home of Otto Frey was built on the old foundation.

In 1879, we find the first mention of the Womens' Benevolent Society, which later became the Ladies Aid Society, and is now the W.S.C.S. (Womens' Society of Christian Service). The first President of the Society was Mrs. James Paine, and Mrs. Barnum was Secretary and

Treasurer. The ladies were apparently as active then as now, as mention is made of a Strawberry Festival on June 10, 1879, and a Peach Festival a little later in the summer. They also packed a barrel of used clothing for the Five Points Mission in New York City. Rev. Elsden conducted a revival while he was here, and thirty-four persons joined the church. In 1880-1881, the Church was served by Robert Kay, and in 1882-1884, by M.M. Curtiss. The present parsonage next to the Church was purchased while Rev. Curtiss was pastor. He was so anxious that the Church have this property for a parsonage that he bought the one that the church had purchased a few years earlier and lived there after he retired. While he was here twenty-six more members joined the church.

One method of raising money for the Church that has not been heard of in recent years was the Donation Social. Printed invitations to the Social to be held at a member's home were sent to all members of the Church. During the evening the members would make a donation to the Church for the minister's salary. One such social, held for Rev. Elsden on January 7, 1879, brought in $102 for his salary. Another event was the "Pound Party," usually given when a new minister arrived at the parsonage. On a selected evening soon after his arrival the members would appear at the parsonage, each bringing a pound of something for the minister's pantry. Sunday School picnics also made their appearance at about this time. Mention is made of one on September 12, 1879. The Church was becoming the center of social life as well as spiritual life. Some members, though, were not always satisfied with the sermons. In an old diary the following was found: "Went to Church and heard another poor sermon. Our poor souls are starving for food and we qet only husks".

In 1885, Gustav Laass was pastor; 1886-1887, D.M. Powell; 1888-1892, William H. Peters. The schedule of services at this time was: Gaylordsville at 10:30 a.m.; on alternate Sundays Ore Hill or Sherman Center at 3 p.m., and at Bulls Bridge at 7:30 p.m. The minister's horse and carriage had to be kept in good shape. During Rev. Peters' stay the church was remodeled. A center aisle and level floor was put in, and a lower pulpit platform, part of which was used for the choir. Before this the choir had been in the balcony at the rear of the church.

Rev. Peters was the first minister to serve the church five years, which was the limit set by the Conference at that time. It was during his stay, in 1890, that the Epworth League was first organized. The Chapter was numbered 3192. The first project tackled by the thirteen charter members was to start Sunday evening devotional meetings. These meetings were at first held in the parsonage, later in the church. As the membership grew and the activities of the League increased, the need was felt for a more appropriate place for their socials and other events.

From 1893-1894, Rev. C. H. Keep was pastor, and during this time a fund was started by the League to build a meeting room that met their needs better. At the start it seemed an almost impossible task. All during the pastorate of John H. Lam, who was here from 1895-1897, the building fund was added to, as it was during the pastorate of James A. Hurn, who was here in 1898. Rev. Hurn became so interested in the young people's work that he married one of the young ladies, Agnes Barnum.

In 1899 and 1900 Charles B. Conro filled the pulpit, and from 1901-1902, Edward H. Roys. In 1903, Robert Elsden made a return visit, and in 1904-1907, Edmund T. Byles. It was in 1904, after ten years of effort, that it was decided that the building fund was large enough to make a start. The work was begun and successfully carried out. Subscriptions and gifts from members of the church and community helped handsomely, and a very satisfactory parlor and kitchen were built on the rear of the church, where they have been very useful and helpful to all the community.

Another social achievement of the Epworth League was the staring of the New England Supper, in November, 1890. At first a program was held in the church and supper in the parsonage. Upon the completion of the parlors, the suppers were held there. From the start it was an annual affair, and has continued almost without interruption to the present time, though it is now called the "Chicken Pie Supper". The program in the church was finally given up but the supper continues.

When the church was remodeled in the early 1890's, the League was not behind in their share. New pulpit furniture was purchased by them, as well as other smaller items. A sum of money was also given each year to the general expenses of the church.

An old diary states that "on December 24, 1905, in this church, Amos Page preached his first sermon." At that time a member of this church, upon becoming a full-time minister, Rev. Page joined the Advent Church, but was always willing to lend a helping hand by filling the pulpit in the absence of the minister.

In 1907-1908, Orville Van Keuren served the church until his death. He was followed from 1908-1910, by James Van Burkelow. The Womens' Benevolent Society was now being called the Ladies Aid Society. In 1910, a Ladies Aid Sale was held. This may or may not have been the first one, but they have been held almost annually ever since. From 1910-1913, Samuel Galloway was pastor and from 1913-1916, Robert Maclaren. The written history of the first Epworth League ends with 1915, and either then or soon afterward the League became inactive.

Mrs. Byles' Sunday School Class: Back row: Esther Jones, Howard Evans, Anna Ferris, Roy Newton, Anna Kennedy (Walden), Henry Thompson, Dorothy Newton, Clarence Gilbert.

Second Row: Gladys Hall, Hattie Brown, Florence Ward, Mrs. Byles and Dorothy, Ruth Hatch, Ethel Bossil, Caroline Brown (Jennings.)

Front Row: Julia Carlson, Steve Joyce, Evelyn Gilbert (Grisell), George Ward, Ruby Hall (Hills.)

From 1916-1919, Issac Stafford was minister here. It was during his stay that the General Conference put Gaylordsville back in the New York East Conference. From 1919-1920, Henry McCullum; 1920, Rev. Lathbury, whose sister wrote the hymn "Break Thou the Bread of Life". Rev. Lathbury was not used to life in the country, and was so discontented here that he resigned after a few months. Rev. Edward Herrick, a retired Congregational minister living in Sherman, filled the pulpit for the rest of the Conference year.

The minister from 1921-1927 was Harry Studwell. During his stay, in 1922, the men of the church dug a small cellar under part of the church and installed a furnace. This did away with the two stoves that had been in the back of the church with the stove pipes running all the way to the front. Also during Rev. Studwell's pastorate, in 1925, the one hundredth anniversary of the church was celebrated. Services were held three evenings and all day Sunday. Some of the speakers were Rev. Amos Page, Dr. William Kidd, District Superintendent, and Rev. Phillip Dodd. Many former residents and former ministers returned for the occasion.

In 1927, Asa Fuller was appointed as pastor and served until 1934. Soon after he came here he set about to reorganize the Epworth League. This new League was just as active as its forerunner. They had been organized only a short time when they decided to put a bathroom in the parsonage. A fund was started to finance the task. Plays were given, as well as suppers and other activities. In 1933 the bathroom was installed, along with a pressure water system. Some of the members did almost all of the work. The League continued to be quite active for several years, taking part in the work of the church and contributing to its support. It again became inactive in 1949. The money left in its treasury was used to purchase a baptismal font.

From 1934 to 1941 Robert Thomas was appointed to serve the church. During the years of the depression the church found its financial problems increased. Several times at Quarterly Conference meetings the question of joining the church with another was discussed. Each time, however, the members put up such a protest, usually accompanied by the promise of a small raise in the minister's salary, that the action was never taken.

From 1941 to 1943, Charles Gray was the pastor, and from 1943-1946, Charles Simpson. In 1946, Arthur Ball was appointed pastor and served the community well. He was reappointed in 1947, but was taken seriously ill and was unable to continue. From September, 1947 to August 1948, Rev. Amos Page, who had retired from his own church, served as supply pastor. Following World War II, rising prices made it impossible for the church to support a full-time minister, and most of the time since then the pulpit has been filled by student ministers. From 1948-1950, Allistare Sellars, who later became a Congregational minister; from 1950-1952, Robert Brashares. Rev. Brashares' father was a Methodist Bishop and this church was honored several times by his being present and delivering the message.

From 1952-1953, Irwin Trotter. Rev. Trotter was ordained in this church on November 23, 1952, by Bishop Baker, of California, who was a friend of his father. In 1954 and 1955, Richard Rice. Rev. Rice followed the example of some of his forerunners and married a local girl, Nancy Booth. In 1955, Rev. Albert Cann, who had retired, agreed to serve this church one year. He was followed by Robert Byrd in 1956, Richard Babcock in 1957, Rev. Schueler in 1958, Alfred Clater in 1959-60, and Thomas Dicken from 1961-1963. Due to the fact that most of these ministers were students and were only in the community on weekends, and moved on as soon as they completed their studies, it was very difficult for them to develop continuing programs that would build up the church. Some attempts were made to reorganize a young people's group, but were unsuccessful until Rev. Dicken formed a small group into the Methodist Youth Fellowship, as it is now called.

In 1963, one of the church's own members, Charles Ward, who had been studying for the ministry, received his license to preach, and was appointed to this church as pastor. The church was again feeling the need for more space, particularly for the Sunday School. Other improvements were needed. Rev. Ward's enthusiasm spurred the members to adopt an overall plan that included an oil furnace to heat the sanctuary, redecorating the sanctuary, indoor toilets, additional Sunday School classrooms, a more satisfactory water supply, moving the furnace for the Sunday School rooms to the cellar, and hot water and other improvements to the kitchen. A Building Fund was started to accomplish these objectives.

In 1965, a memorial bequest paid for drilling an artesian well to serve both the church and the parsonage. In 1966, an oil furnace was installed in the church cellar, and in 1967, just before Rev. Ward completed his pastorate, the sanctuary was completely redecorated. These two steps were paid for with accumulated interest from the church trust funds.

In 1964, The Ladies' Summer Sale was expanded into the Church Fair, held on the nearby Firemen's Field. Though small at the start it has grown and was expanded again in 1968 to include a chicken barbeque.

In 1967, John Bachetti came as pastor. That fall it was decided that, although the building fund was not large enough to pay for all of the project, it should be started as the Sunday School classrooms were badly needed. In January, 1968, a mild spell permitted the cellar to be dug and the foundation laid. Work progressed through the winter, and the addition, containing three classrooms, two lavatories and a full basement was completed in the spring. Hot water was also installed in the kitchen, completing all of the steps in the overall plan adopted four years previously. The new rooms were dedicated by Dr. Kirkland, District Superintendent, on June 2, with over 100 members, friends and former ministers present. $6,500 had been borrowed to complete the project, and more than one-half of it was repaid in less than one year.

In 1971, Roy Jacobsen was appointed here. At that time Gaylordsville was "yoked" with the New Fairfield Church, which meant that one minister served both churches. After that Jeffrey Fillian, Craig Fitzsimmons, James Smith, and Lori Miller served as pastors, followed by Paul Hibbard, Marion Hubbard, and followed by a succession of part-time ministers.

THE BAPTIST CHURCH

After a series of revival meetings held in the schoolhouse in 1824, several members of the community felt that they would favor the Baptist Church over the other denominations that were to be represented in the village. The nearest Baptist Churches were in New Milford and Wingdale and getting to them was sometimes difficult. In 1838, the Baptists felt that, even though the New Milford Baptist minister came up once in a while and held services in the Union meeting house, the time had come for them to have their own Church Society.

On March 21, 1838, a Council meeting was held in the Union Meeting House to organize the Baptists into "The Gaylord's Bridge

Baptist Church." Delegates were present from Dover, Danbury and New Milford. Six men and twelve women joined the new church. They were: Samuel Goodsell, Jesse Hallock, Jabez Covil, Alvah H. Buck, Truman Bailey, David Whitehead, Rebecca Tibbets, Lucretia Goodsell, Martha Halleck, Elizabeth Tibbets, Mercy Kellogg, Lucretia A. Buck, Laura Bailey, Maria Bailey, Ann Covil, Sally Covil, Susan Marsh, and Sarah Goodsell. Eight others joined soon after the church was formed.

The first minister of the new church was Elder Elijah Baldwin, who was to preach "one half of the time" as services were held every other Sunday in the Union Meeting House. Attendance at these services was closely watched, and any member not attending three services in a row was called upon by a committee and asked to give his reasons for not attending. One man so called upon gave as his reason for staying away that the last time he went to church the minister read his sermon.

In May, 1843, Edwin Bailey was engaged to preach one-half of the time for one year, and in 1844, Amos Benedict; 1846, Seth Higby; 1848, Henry M. Barlow. At this time some of the church meetings were being held in the Village Institute which was located on the west side of the river almost directly across the road from where the Methodist Church is now located. On February 10, 1849, the church was reorganized, using the same name, and adopting a constitution. The association was made up of all of the male members of the church over twenty-one years old. This maneuver excluded the women of the church from the business or "covenant meetings." The annual meeting of the church was set as the first Monday of each December.

In 1850, Amos Benedict returned as pastor. From 1852-1866 no records of the church activities were kept. In 1866, Elder Hepburn was acting as pastor. In 1867, Rev. Denison. On February 23, 1868, the church was reorganized again under the name "The Baptist Society of Gaylordsville." Another gap in the records ends on April 15, 1876. At that time the pulpit was being filled by Rev. D.F. Chapman. The Baptists seem to have purchased the Village Institute, as it was then being called the Chapel.

In March, 1877, on the recommendation of the council, the members voted to change the name of the church to "The Second Baptist Church of New Milford." In 1878, the records showed a total of eighteen members, a decrease of one from the previous year. Mention was also made of a Sunday School. At a church meeting held on October 18, 1879, the following members in good standing were elected: Trustees: E.S. Merwin, B.E. Monroe, John Bates, M.E. Hendrix, J.E. Hepburn, E.A. Bailey, and E.G. Merwin. The last entry in the first and only known record book is dated April 10, 1880. On that day the retiring clerk turned over all records, cash, and papers to the new clerk, Bennett E. Monroe.

THE ORATORY OF THE LITTLE WAY

The Oratory Of The Little Way on South Kent Road in Gaylordsville is a non-denominational retreat house. The Oratory was founded in 1967 by the Rev. Benjamin Priest, an Episcopal clergyman, who subsidized it with his own funds. Father Priest called it the Oratory Of The Little Way after St. Therese of Lisieux, who believed in ordinary holiness. The Oratory is managed under the auspices of the Episcopal Church but is open to all people who need spiritual and physical healing. Following the death of Father Priest, the Oratory was run by Reverend George Hall and his wife, Beverly, as a retreat center. When they moved away, Nigel Mumford was installed as a lay director of the healing ministry and retreat center. Following Nigel Mumford's tenure, there were various directors, the present director being Bishop Alexander McCullough. The Oratory operates on donations from visitors who use the facilities.

THE POST OFFICE

The Post Office was first established here in May, 1826. Peter Gaylord was the first Postmaster and had the office, called Gaylords Village, in his store. At that time both the Poughkeepsie and Albany stages passed through the village and the mail was delivered by them to post offices all along the route. Sylvanus Merwin was appointed Postmaster on December 8, 1838, and was reappointed in 1840 when the name was changed to Ousatonic. Mr. Merwin had a hotel and store west of the river, and the post office was moved there. Peter Gaylord was again appointed on June 30, 1841, and moved the office back to his store. He had the name changed again, this time to Gaylords Bridge. John Gaylord received the appointment on February 9, 1842.

In 1853, Sylvanus Merwin was again made the Postmaster. He now had a hotel by the railroad, so the post office was located there. He also had the name changed to Merwinsville, a name the railroad used for many years on the station. John Gaylord got the appointment again in 1861 and the office went back to the Gaylord store. This time the name was changed to Gaylordsville. Merwin was again appointed in 1867 and took the office back to his hotel, but the Post Office Department rebelled at changing the name so often, and it remained Gaylordsville.

Alexander Barlow became postmaster in 1869 and had the office in his store, which was across the street from the Gaylord store. The mail was now coming on the train, and had to be carried between the post office and the station, usually by a man on foot. The mail in those days was mostly letters, so the load was not heavy. One of the reasons for building the footbridge across the valley to the station was to shorten the trip for the mail carrier. Some of the early carriers were N. Kellogg, Robert Lane, John Gaylord, and Edmond Hatch. With the advent of parcel post and newspapers and magazines by mail, a horse and wagon had to be used.

Short cut bridge to the station along a proposed railroad to a marble quarry, one-quarter mile north of the center of town; it was used a long time for mail carried on foot from the station to the post office in the village.

All the Gaylordsville residents had to go to the post office to pick up their mail. Some had individual post office boxes while others had their mail go into General Delivery. Gaylordsville would not have rural delivery for the Village until the 1980's.

In February, 1902, a rural delivery route was established from Gaylordsville to cover most of the town of Sherman. The first rural carrier was Howard Conkrite, who covered the thirty-six miles either on horseback or with a horse and two-wheeled cart. He carried the mail for two years, and was followed by John Roche, who kept the job for over thirty years, using at first an enclosed wagon, or a sleigh in the winter. When both roads and cars had improved, he switched to Fords. He retired in 1934.

John Roche was the rural carrier from 1904 to 1934

It was desirable to have the Post Office located at your store as it brought in customers. The Postmaster was a political appointment and changed with each election or change of political party until Edward Honan. Both political parties agreed that the Post Office should stay at his store.

In 1912, Edward Honan became Postmaster and the office was again returned to its original place in Peter Gaylord's store, as Mr. Honan had purchased the store several years earlier. The Sherman Post Office had been discontinued by this time, increasing the work of the Gaylordsville postmaster and rural carrier. For many years while Mr. Honan was postmaster, Clarence Evans took the mail to the station.

Postmaster Edward Honan handing mail to Clarence Evans

During the late 1920's and all through the thirties the passenger and mail trains did not stop at Gaylordsville. The pouch of first class mail was hung on a frame that allowed it to be caught by a hook that swung out from the mail car. The parcel post was sent on the milk train to New Milford where it was transferred to the next express. The sacks of incoming mail were pushed from the train as it sped past and were sometimes scattered for some distance along the track or rolled down the embankment, making the carrier's task more difficult. In the spring of 1942 the trains resumed their stop at Gaylordsville, and the mail could be handled more easily.

Following Mr. Roche's retirement, the rural carriers during Mr. Honan's term in office were two temporary carriers, David Duryea and Harold Dwy. In 1937, Thomas Honan became the regular carrier. He was followed by two more temporary carriers, Marshall Munch of Sherman, 1942-45; and Clark Anderson, 1945-51. In 1946, Mr. Honan retired and his son Thomas became acting postmaster and then postmaster. In February, 1949, a post office was again established in Sherman, and soon afterward the rural route was transferred there.

The population of Gaylordsville was growing, and Peter Gaylord's store, 150 years old, was no longer adequate for the increased trade. A new store was built a short distance to the north. When the business was moved into the new building in May, 1952, the post office was also moved.

In 1956, the Post Office Department ended its policy of sending the mail for this area by train, and started using trucks, thus doing away with the trip from the post office to the station. The last man to have that job was Jay Grisell. In 1970, Thomas Honan retired, and Mrs. Mabel Honan took over the post office.

The name of the Post Office Dept. changed to the U.S. Postal Service. An addition was built onto the store for the post office to move into. Mabel Honan retired in 1984, and Rosemarie (Mimi) Burkhardt, was then appointed Postmaster.

The rural route was established for Gaylordsville deliveries, with John Blank as the first carrier. Barbara Thorland worked as clerk for twenty-four years. Postmaster Burkhardt's car license plate was 06755, the zip code for the Gaylordsville Post Office. After working thirty-one years at the post office, she retired in 2006 and Meg Luddy was appointed the new Postmaster.

Present personnel include the Postmaster, 1 part-time clerk, a rural carrier, and substitute carrier. They deliver 4,000 pieces of mail daily to 780 addresses from the Gaylordsville, CT post office. The rural route covers thirty-three miles each day, six days a week. The post office needed more space to operate and moved one half mile south on Kent Road (Route 7) to George Washington Plaza in July of 2006, where Meg Luddy continued as Postmaster. Following her transfer to another office, Kevin Peatfield was appointed Postmaster.

THE STATION HOTEL AND THE RAILROAD

The history of the hotel begins in 1837, when surveyors for the Housatonic Railroad were looking for the best route up the valley through Gaylordsville. They spent a few nights in the hotel, west of the river that was run by Sylvanus Merwin, who was a shrewd business man. During their evening conversation they discussed their day's work, and Mr. Merwin was able to learn the exact path the rails would follow. With an eye to the future he bought land east of the village through which the railroad must pass, and started building a second hotel there. When the lawyers for the railroad arrived to negotiate for a right-of-way through his property, Mr. Merwin was in a position to bargain. He insisted that they agree to use the hotel as a meal stop for all passenger trains, and the station must be called Merwinsville. The railroad needed the land, and the hotel, being somewhat midway between the ends of the proposed line, Bridgeport and Pittsfield, would make an excellent meal stop, so they agreed to the terms. When the first train arrived in 1843, the hotel was ready. An addition was built on the south end of the hotel to house the ticket office and waiting rooms, and the insatiable Merwin became the station agent.

Mr. Merwin seems to have been determined to make the hotel area a center of activity. He built a store south of the hotel, and a schoolhouse north of it. The store was run by a Mr. Graves, who was related to Mrs. Merwin. The school was for girls, some of whom probably boarded in the hotel, but local girls also attended.

Merwin's Hotel was unique for its time - a large and gracious hotel in the foothills of northwest Connecticut. The three-story structure was architecturally interesting with a nine-column Georgian exterior, latticed balconies, and ample windows. Inside, the four first-floor dining rooms were tastefully decorated. The food was brought up from the basement kitchen and bakery on a dumbwaiter. The trains only stopped for twenty minutes so everything had to be ready when they arrived. Some of the cooking was done by Mrs. Merwin, but they also employed a chef, Edward Hallock. Mr. Hallock was a colorful character. He always wore a skull cap and carried his pipe and tobacco in a large pouch. He made his own clothes, and it was not unusual to see him in brightly colored calico trousers. Today's "mod" clothes would have been just his style. When speaking of Mr. and Mrs. Merwin - to someone else he usually referred to them as the "old rooster and the old hen".

Water for the kitchen came from a spring on the hillside to the east. There was also a wash stand in the station and one on the second floor. A watering trough across the drive also was kept full by the spring.

From the ground floor of the hotel four stairways merged in a center landing from where two stairways continued to the second floor. Here were the bedrooms and a lounge. Three doors led to the balcony that stretched the full length of the building. This was the first floor porch that had six doors leading into the station and dining rooms.

Two narrow steep, stairways led up to the third floor. Here a grand ballroom provided room for dances and weekend entertainment. The Harvey Girls performed there in the 1890's and square dances drew farmers and their families from the surrounding countryside. The ballroom ran the whole length of the main building, and was lined on both sides with small dressing rooms. Three chandeliers provided light for the dancers. Across the road a long shed provided shelter for their horses.

The hotel was also a stop for the east-west stage, providing a connection to many points, and adding to the activity. The stage arrived on Stagecoach Road, which ran just north of the schoolhouse. It then entered the area east of the hotel and had to make a u-turn before leaving. This area was not a public road at that time, and was closed at night by a gate near the school.

But the grand days of the Merwinsville Hotel could not last. In 1858 ten or twelve customers could be expected from each train for the fifty-cent meals in addition to the train crew, who apparently ate free. In the 1870's, however, the advent of the railroad dining car made the meal stop unnecessary and the contract was terminated in 1877.

Merwin's son-in-law, Ed Hurd, had taken over as station agent. He had been telegraph operator in Shelton while the Merwin's daughter was the operator at Merwinsville. They became acquainted by telegraph, and eventually she became Mrs. Hurd. Upon Mr. Merwin's death in 1884, at the age of 82, the Hurds became owners of the hotel.

Station Agent Ed Hurd and Mrs. Hurd at left of picture

They tried several ways to increase business. Summer boarders helped for a while, as did dinner dances held in the ballroom. In 1890 an oyster dinner and dancing to the music of a band from Bridgeport cost the invited guest $1.25. In spite of his efforts, however, the hotel seemed doomed. First the school closed. Then the store, which Edward Honan had taken over from Mr. Graves, was closed in 1901 when Mr. Honan purchased the store built by Peter Gaylord. Mr. Hurd finally closed the hotel as a losing venture, but continued as station agent, with John Bandzura helping with the freight.

9:17 a.m. train. Dr. Dolan shown boarding train

Around 1905 the railroad informed Mr. Hurd that they were going to replace him with a younger man. Mr. Hurd informed them that if they were getting a new agent they would have to get a new station also, as they could not use his without him. They took him at his word, and built a ticket office on the end of the freight house, which was about fifty yards down the track. Mr. Bandzura acted as agent until the new man, Frank Odlum arrived. Bandzura then took over the station at South Kent, which the railroad called Woodrow. In 1915 the old freight house was torn down and replaced with a combination passenger station and freight house. On February 1, 1918, the station was renamed Gaylordsville. The agents that followed were: Edward Shea, Hardy Noyer, Ezra Atkins, Mr. Towey, and John Lynch.

Soon after the ticket office left the hotel the building was purchased in 1916 by Michael Hastings, a railroad section foreman. The Hastings used the ground floor as an apartment. One of the former waiting rooms became their kitchen. Several years later their son James married and had an apartment upstairs. They occupied the hotel until 1947.

No one lived in the building after that. Mr. Hastings was a carpenter and had a shop in the rooms that had housed the railroad station. For a number of years the fire department used the former dining rooms for storing their carnival materials. The building was purchased by Edward Dolan and used in much the same manner. A fire in the building in 1970 ended its use for both of these purposes and it became completely vacant, prey to souvenir hunters.

For a number of years one resident of Gaylordsville had been trying to promote the idea of restoring the hotel to its former grandeur. George Haase had purchased a home on Riverview Road near the former lumberyard, and not far from the hotel. It was not until the summer of 1971 that he got anyone to listen to his plans. Gerald Nahley, the new owner of Honan's Market, was one of the first to respond, and together the two recruited townspeople to join in the project, and thus the Merwinsville Hotel Restoration was born.

Though disreputable to look at, the building was found to be structurally sound. The owner, Mr. Dolan, agreed to sell it to the Merwinsville Hotel Restoration, a non-profit corporation, for the sum of $1.00. (This was $1.00 more than the group had in their treasury!) Its officers were George Haase, John Flynn, Gerald Nahley, Barbara Thorland, and Elwin Smith. Once the project got underway many local residents responded enthusiastically. Fund raising projects were held and donations received. Morris House Movers jacked and leveled the building so work on the foundations could proceed.

Over the years much has been accomplished at the hotel. There is now a finished basement with a fully stocked wine cellar.

The first floor parlor on the north end is furnished with period antiques. On the south end of the first floor the station waiting room has been recreated with much authentic railroad memorabilia including a stove used on a railway caboose, as well as freight ledgers and railway documents. There is a post office box section from the early Gaylordsville Post Office donated by former Postmaster Mabel Honan. On the south end of the second floor there is a completed apartment, which is rented, thus providing an on-premises caretaker for the building.

A new heating system has been installed in the building, as well as an office and storage area on the second floor. Long-range plans call for restoration of the 3rd floor ballroom.

THE POWER HOUSE

Shortly after 1900, a new industry came to Gaylordsville. A group of men formed the New Milford Electric Company and began work on a power plant about a mile north of the village. A dam on the Housatonic River was built about a mile upstream from the power house, in Bulls Bridge, a few hundred feet north of the covered bridge. It formed a reservoir four miles long, reaching all the way to Kent. The dam was over 200 feet long in a horseshoe shape, reinforced in the center by a natural rock formation. While it was being built the river was diverted to the west in a channel that was later closed off by what is known as the Spooner Dam.

The canal to carry the water to the power house was also a tremendous project, employing hundreds of men, thirty teams of horses, derricks, pile drivers, and a little railroad that was laid in the bed of the canal as it was dug.

For part of the way, the bank of the canal was made of carefully laid blocks of stone, while in other places it was blasted out of solid rock. It traveled nearly two miles by a level water route to reach the power house a mile from the dam. It ended about 100 feet above the river. Gates at both ends controlled the flow of water. At first one penstock, later two, carried the water down the hillside to the plant. After it turned the generators, it re-entered the Housatonic River.

This was the largest hydro-electric plant built up to that time. For many years all of the power produced here went to Waterbury. Gaylordsville, only a mile away, remained without electricity for over ten years until the Wemanesa Grange took the lead in promoting the Gaylordsville Electric Company. This company built a power line to the plant, purchased the electricity and sold it to the residents, at first only in the center, but gradually expanding to reach most of the village. The company later sold out to the Connecticut Light and Power Company, which also purchased the dam, canal, and power plant from the New Milford Electric Company. During the 1960's, when there was a surplus of power available from newer plants, this plant was only used during peak hours, and there was some talk of closing it altogether. A few years later, demands for electricity increased and soon this plant was again running at capacity.

The project is now over 100 years old, and continues to make power in much the same way that it did originally. With more recent technology, manpower staffing at both the headgate house near the dam, and at the powerhouse have been replaced with computer controls. This once required 3 operators, 3 assistant operators, and 3 headgate operators, 24 hours/day, 7 days/week. With these and other technical improvements over time, the project continues to run with most of the original major equipment.

WEMANESA GRANGE NO. 170

The Grange in Gaylordsville was organized on March 9, 1908, at the home of Charles Evans. Mr. Vincent and Mr. Johnson of the Kent Grange came down and helped with the ceremony. There were twenty-six charter members as follows: Mr. and Mrs. Charles Evans, Clarence

Evans, Mr. and Mrs. W.B. Hungerford, Mr. and Mrs. John Paine, Mary Paine, Mr. and Mrs. Henry Pomeroy, Charles Pomeroy, Mr. and Mrs. Edward Austin, Thomas Austin, Genevieve Austin, Mr. and Mrs. Frank Ward, Florence Ward, Mr. and Mrs. William Thompson, Dr. and Mrs. Dolan, Mr. and Mrs. George Newton, Mr. and Mrs. Alphonso Hyde. The first Master was W.B. Hungerford, and the first Overseer, Charles Evans.

For a time the meetings were held in the parlors of the Methodist Church, and the membership soon grew to over one hundred. The first project was to build a grange hall. A committee was appointed to select a site. After considering several they chose one west of the river not far from the church. The building of the hall was in charge of Newton Weaver, who worked without pay, as did many of the members. One member donated some logs, which other members cut and hauled to the saw mill at the Flynn farm, where they were sawed into timbers for the frame of the building. When completed the hall had cost about $2,550, and the Grange was in debt for most of it.

In June, 1911, the new hall was dedicated by State Grange Master Healy, and in December, 1920, the balance of the mortgage was paid in full. At the annual supper, March 9, 1921, State Master Blakeman was present to witness the burning of the mortgage and gave the address.

Even before the hall was completed, the women of the Grange were forming a Ladies' Degree Team, and were soon able to work all four degrees. They became well-known in the area, traveling to nearly all of the nearby granges to confer the degrees.

Many of the Grange members, as well as others in the community, had long been annoyed because Gaylordsville was still without electricity, even though the power plant had been only a mile away for many years. The Grange decided to do something about it, and was instrumental in promoting the Gaylordsville Electric Company, purchasing $1000 worth of its stock. Community service has always been one of the leading objectives, and many improvements in the village could be traced back to the Grange.

The Grange has always had its ups and downs, as most organizations do. At times there have been so few interested members that it was difficult to carry on, but always the faithful few have kept things going until an influx of new members would give it a lift. The Sherman Grange closed, and several members who wished to continue their grange work transferred their membership to Wemanesa. For a number of years a Junior Grange was sponsored which won state honors. Those who have held the office of Master are: W.B. Hungerford, Charles Evans, George Newton, Charles Soule, Edwin Haring, Paul Newton, Ella Conkrite, George Strid, Wesley Pomeroy, Norman Wyble, James Trotter, Thomas J. Dodd, John Flynn, Fred Pettes, William Lang, Gertrude Wyble, Albert Bandy, Andrew Morren, Elwin Smith, Jerome Deeds, and Janet Judd.

In 1971 the number of interested members dropped so low that those remaining decided that it would no longer be practical to maintain the Grange Hall. Arrangements were made with the church to return to the original practice of holding the Grange meetings in the church parlors. This was started in November, and the Grange Hall put up for sale. It was purchased by a Mr. Carmellini and then by Gail and Mark Estabrooks and made into an antique mall, called the Bittersweet Shop.

Virginia (Ginny) Hastings Smith moved to the Merwinsville Hotel in 1931, when she was 6 years old, along with her parents, Nora and Jim Hastings. She grew up there and wrote of her memories of living in that old building and life in Gaylordsville as it was then. She attended the Waller District School for grades 1 through 3, and the Gaylord District School for grades 4 through 6. She then attended Jr. High and 4 years of high school in New Milford, graduating in 1944. She was graduated from the Bridgeport School Of Nursing in 1947. Ginny married Elwin (Al) Smith in 1949. They had 4 daughters: Debbie, Marcia, Carol and Joanne, and an adopted son, Douglas. After her marriage both Ginny and Al were very active Wemanesa Grange members. Due to the declining grange membership, the Wemanesa Grange gave up their charter, with the final meeting being held in 1992. Ginny Smith compiled the history of Wemanesa Grange #170, Gaylordsville, Connecticut, using information taken from secretarial notes of grange meetings and various other documents, starting from July, 1909, and continuing until 1992. A copy of this history is now at the Connecticut Historical Society in Hartford.

Scouts

The Gaylordsville troops of the Boy Scouts and the Campfire Girls were organized at about the same time. The Scouts organized in 1914, and were known as Troop III, New Milford at Gaylordsville, the Moose Patrol. Under the leadership of Dr. Henry Turrill a group of seven boys, Vincent Dolan, Harold Newton, Robert McClaren, Robert Jones, Fred Waller, Ronald Disbrow and Paul Newton formed the original Moose Patrol. They were soon joined by Theodore Carlson, Roy Allen, Albert Travers and Wally Anderson.

The Moose Patrol

Camp sites were maintained on Liberty Hill and at Cedar Hill, where many of their scouting activities were carried out. Dr. Turrill moved to Kent and started another troop there. Ronald Disbrow became leader of the Moose Patrol, and the two troops sometimes went on hikes and camping trips together, with contests between the two troops. They remained active for several years.

The Campfire Girls were started in 1915. Nineteen girls had Bessie Cornwell as their leader. They made use of the Boy Scout campsites on Cedar Hill and Liberty Hill for their outdoor activities. They also had indoor projects, cooking, sewing and homemaking. A special project that some of the girls did was to prepare a group of younger girls to become Campfire Girls when they became old enough. They were called Bluebirds.

Sitting: …Ferris, Florence Boinay, Elizabeth Honan and Esther Newton. The older girls kneeling are: Cora Ferris, Mary Newton, Alta Hall, Blanche Pomeroy, and Grace Thompson. Standing: Marjorie Roberts, Bessie Cornwell,…. Fredlund, Alice Boinay, Elsie Carlson, Bessie Carlson and Minnie Dwy.

The next attempt at scouting was not made until 1960, when a Cub Scout troop was started with Mrs. Marshall Beatty and Mrs. Elmer Carlson as Den Mothers. This troop lasted for about five years.

Cub Scouts, 1960. Rosemary Beatty, Den Mother, Alden Beatty, David Flynn, Kenneth Carlson, Peter Steinman, and Timothy Cole.

Girl Scout troop 277 with leaders Rosemary Nahley, Sue DeBoy, and Mimi Burkhardt started in 1972 with Brownies from Gaylordsville. It continued to be active until 1980. The meetings were held weekly at the Gaylordsville United Methodist Church hall. The girls performed community service such as planting flowers by the Gaylordsville town sign, playing bingo with the elderly, caroling during the holidays for the home-bound, and delivering cookies that the girls had made. They went on many camp-outs and trips to New York City.

In the early 1980's there was renewed interest in girl scouting in Gaylordsville. There were a handful of girls who spanned different ages and different grades in school. They came together as one troop. Over the years, during the 1980's and 1990's as Gaylordsville's population grew so did girl scouting in Gaylordsville. Soon there were Brownie Girl Scout troops for first, second and third grades, as well as Junior and Cadet Troops. The Gaylordsville Girl Scouts met at the Gaylordsville Methodist Church and were active in the Gaylordsville community as well as the New Milford community. Some of their local activities included placing flags on local veterans' graves at the Gaylord and Morningside Cemeteries, singing Christmas carols at the Gaylordsville Rest Home and helping the residents there decorate their tree with ornaments the girls made. They also baked goodies for the annual tree lighting and marched in the Memorial Day parade. Some of the women who guided these young girls included Sue Powers, Maureen Mertens, Michele Deeds, Fran Kelly, Sue Monte, Maureen Manwaring, Kay Stietzel, Stephanie Hastings, Kathy Martin, Annetta Muir, Suzan Dahl, Debbie Wirag and Valerie Loorman.

Left to right, back row: Melissa Jewell, Katie Muir, Dana Thomas, Lisa DeLuca, Jennifer Schonoff, Andrea Stier, Michelle Dahl, and Amanda Ward. Middle row: Sarah Baldi, Anne Mertens, Ashley Hamilton, Beth Potter, Joyce Ward, Lyndsey Bennett, Heidi Gantner, and Kathleen Hastings. Front row: Veena Panduranga and Hannah Flynn. Missing from the photo are: Jessica Miller and Jennifer Haber.

Another Boy Scout troop led by Al Burkhardt became active in 1975. The boys met once each week during school months. They did many outdoor activities, such as ice fishing, making maple syrup, and touring the train yards of Waterbury. They went on many hikes and camp-outs. One camp-out was held in the old Merwinsville Hotel before it was restored. The sounds of the old building in the middle of the night and ghost stories that were told fed the young imaginations. The troop lasted from Cub Scouts and Webelos Scouts until Boy Scouts when it transferred to a New Milford Troop. The troop members were Jack Tracey, Matthew Brothers, Tim O'Hara, Maury Menard, John Burkhardt, and Stephen Nahley.

The pavilion located at Emanuel Williamson Park, off Kent Road (Route 7), was the Eagle Scout project of John Burkhardt. In 1987 he sent letters to all the residents of Gaylordsville requesting donations of money and volunteers. Many helped in the planning and constructing of the pavilion. It was made with a telephone pole frame and paved floor. Al Stietzel supervised the construction of the roof. The park pavilion was dedicated at a Gaylordsville town picnic. The second time that the pavilion was used was on the occasion of John Burkhardt's Eagle Scout ceremony with Connecticut State Senator, M. Adela (Dell) Eads and 67th District Representative Oskar Rogg present, along with fellow Eagle Scouts and John's Boy Scout Troop 432. The pavilion is still used for picnics in the park.

Betsy Clark was the leader of a group of Senior Scouts who were seen each Christmas helping out and providing activities for children at the Gaylord school house during Christmas open house.

Suzette Berger and Tina Toussaint were the leaders of Troop 324 which consisted of 8 girls: Rachel Berger, Tracey Howard, Danielle Toussaint, Emily Hendrix, Emily Hauser, Samantha Martin, Rachel Urbanowski, and Meghan Bresson. For many years the scouts met at the Gaylordsville United Methodist Church for their activities which included sports and games, singing, arts and crafts, plays and cooking. The girls have progressed from Daisy Scouts to Brownies, then Junior Girl Scouts, Cadets, and Senior Scouts. Some favorite memories the girls talked about were trips they went on to Salem MA, Rocking Horse Dude Ranch, and camping overnight at the zoo. The scouts also helped local organizations fix up homes as well as donate food baskets to needy senior citizens. They marched in many of the Gaylordsville Memorial Day Parades. Each year since 1996 during the week before Memorial

Day the girls of Troop 324 placed the flags on all of the veterans' graves in both Morningside and Gaylord Cemetery.

CIVIL WAR VETERANS

William Warner	Died December 23, 1862	Age 18
Barnett Camp	Died June 5, 1860	Age 23
Edwin Camp	Died May 15, 1867	Age 24
George Brague	Died 1928	Age 81
Alexander Conkrite	Died July 13, 1863	Age 18
James D. Mosher	Died August 6, 1853	Age 22
Andrew Bailey	Died December 20, 1872	Age 32
Curtis Hall	Died 1888	Age 57
Edmund Hatch	Died 1926	Age 85
Charles H. Gaylord	Died 1927	

THE KNITTING CLUB AND
THE WORLD WAR II MEMORIAL

During World War II quite a number of the young men and women of the village were serving in the various branches of the Armed Services. The Army, Navy, Marines, Air Force, and the Merchant Marine all had some men from Gaylordsville in them.

The women left at home, the wives, mothers, and friends of the servicemen, felt that they should be doing something to help out. Although they were serving as airplane spotters, taking first aid courses, and serving in other forms of Civilian Defense, they wanted to do something for the servicemen themselves. They decided to form a Knitting Club. Yarn was purchased in quantity through the Red Cross and distributed to the members who made it into socks, scarves, sweaters and gloves. Every serviceman from Gaylordsville received gifts from the Club and many more were sent to the Red Cross to be given to other men who needed them.

To pay for the yarn, and to meet the other expenses of the Club, the members paid dues and raised money in other ways. When the war was over and the men came home, the Club had some money left in its treasury. They decided to erect a memorial to the thirty-one men and one woman who had served their country in time of war. They decided that a boulder with a plaque mounted on it would be appropriate. Considerable time was spent looking for boulders that would be adaptable to the plaques. One was finally selected from the Page farm in Squash Hollow. Its weight was estimated to be around ten tons, so the Sega Construction firm was engaged to help move it to the triangle at the junction of Routes 7 and 55.

It was finally set to the ladies' satisfaction, and Anton Dvorak was given the job of mounting the plaque. A dedication service was held Sunday afternoon, November 10, 1946. Mrs. James Hastings, president of the Knitting Club, presided over the service. Rev. Arthur Ball, Rev. Father Martin, Rev. John Cuyler, and Rev. Charles Simpson took part in the dedication.

The following spring the Grange erected a flag pole near the memorial and the first flag raising ceremony was held on Memorial Day, 1947. The newly formed Fire Department placed a wreath on the plaque, and later voted to do this every year with an appropriate service. This has been done every year on Memorial Day, with all of the organizations in the community taking part in a short parade ending at the monument. A short service is held, ending with the firing squad and taps. In this way the ones who died in action and those who have since passed away are remembered, and a tribute paid to the veterans of all wars for the services they gave. If it had not been for the foresight of the knitting club, the names of the community servicemen might have been forgotten, but now they are preserved for all to see and remember.

Lifting the stone that was chosen to be the Memorial Rock

Left to right: Art Sega, Harold Dwy, Lowell Hendrix, Emanuel Williamson, Jim Hastings, Jack Dodd, and Clarence Hendrix.

In 1991, when the new bridge was built, the road was re-aligned, necessitating the relocation of the memorial rock to the center of the village. The new location is called the Charlie Jones Memorial Park in honor of the man who was a valuable member of the community.

250ᵗʰ ANNIVERSARY PARADE

One of the shortest lived organizations, but one that accomplished its purpose, was the 250ᵗʰ anniversary parade float committee. When plans were being made for New Milford's 250ᵗʰ anniversary celebration, in 1957, some of Gaylordsville's older residents remembered that in 1907, at the 200ᵗʰ anniversary, Gaylordsville had a float in the parade that was given honorable mention. They suggested that a float be entered again in the 1957 parade. A committee was formed representing all of the organizations in the community. Frank Beach was elected chairman and Elsie Carlson, treasurer.

Plans were drawn for a scale model schoolhouse that would fit on a float. Work was done evenings and weekends, probably with as many bosses as workers, but progress was made. Charles Pomeroy made room in one of his barns at the lumberyard, and the work was done there. When the men finished the construction, the women took over, painting the building and trimming the float with bunting. The morning of the parade the cupola and the flag were added after the float was taken out of the barn and then it was ready to go. Frank Carlson and Steven Sanford drove the tractor. Mrs. Cornwell rode on the float accompanied by some of the children in the last class that she taught. When the parade was over, the Little Red Schoolhouse was awarded second prize.

275ᵗʰ ANNIVERSARY PARADE

In 1982 New Milford celebrated it 275ᵗʰ anniversary with a parade. Gaylordsville took part in this celebration in a big way. Under the direction of Aaron Seltzer, the Gaylordsville Parade Committee chairman, many volunteers worked for nearly a year on building floats, fitting them with buntings and gathering costumes. The main float was a replica of the red schoolhouse built under the direction of Al Stietzel.

During the parade Hattie Anderson, the oldest resident of the village, sat on the float in front of the schoolhouse, surrounded by young children. Another two floats held benches filled with people dressed in period clothing, with a sign reading "Gaylordsville Residents". Teenage girls dressed as suffragettes carried signs depicting the names of various Gaylordsville organizations. Also in the parade was a horse-drawn old fashioned carriage with occupants in top hats dressed in their Sunday best. The three restored antique fire wagons pulled by boys and men, wearing red suspenders and red fire hats, preceded the uniformed Gaylordsville Volunteer Fire Department and their fire trucks. Most of the people of Gaylordsville marched in this parade.

Later the replica of the schoolhouse was placed in the Emmanuel Williamson Park. The ceremony included the burying of a time capsule and a picnic. Eventually the building deteriorated with time and vandalism and it was removed by the town for safety reasons.

Please note the life-like horses in this picture...... they were designed and made by Frank Piliero. The float was actually pulled by a garden tractor.

SOCIAL LIFE IN THE COMMUNITY

The social life of the nineteenth century depended largely on the talents and ingenuity of the villagers. Some projects, such as the Gaylordsville Singing School, were beneficial as well as entertaining. Men and women of all ages came to learn and practice singing in harmony. The Church Choir was much improved by its members that attended the school. Groups from the school also traveled to nearby communities to give concerts. The school was discontinued in the early 1900's.

Another group that was active for a time was "The Gaylordsville Debating Club and Lyceum", sometimes called "The Young Men's Debating Club and Lyceum of Gaylordsville". It was organized in January, 1879, with the purpose, according to the preamble of its Constitution, of "intellectual improvement in disputation and oratory". William H. Graves was the first president, with George Knapp, Harry Edwards, and Bennett Camp on the officers' roll. The members were Minot Giddings, Henry Evans, Arrin Roberts, Irwin Marsh, G.M. Kellogg, Bennett Monroe, Lewis Mosher, John Tibbetts, Earl Stone, Henry Roberts, A.S. Whitney, E.S. Gaylord, William Buckingham, Edwin Hungerford, Gilbert White, Curtis Buck, Cal Erwin, Orra Warner, E.W. Merwin, John Taylor, Henry Piercy, G.W. Marsh, H.W. Deull, Andrew Evans, Andrew Bailey, and John Hepburn. Meetings were held every Friday evening during the fall and winter. The meetings were open to the public, but only the members could take part in the debates, being chosen two weeks in advance. All sorts of subjects were debated, including politics, religion and social problems. If the debate ended too soon, one of the members would be called upon to give an oration on his favorite subject. The club flourished for a number of years, sometimes varying its routine with an out-of-town speaker or a magic lantern show. Whether or not it accomplished its purpose of "intellectual improvement" is perhaps itself debatable, but at least it provided an evening's entertainment each week.

The church socials and neighborhood socials also provided entertainment. Some of those planning to attend were asked to be prepared to perform. It could be a musical selection, monologue, poem, skit, or almost any sort of number. John Paine, invited to a social in 1898, recited this original poem:

Within you will find the poem
At our last social read
It was ground out at the mill
Which was by John Paine fed.

In it neither wit nor wisdom
Which you surely knew before
Written by a country bumpkin
Only that and nothing more.

Seated in my humble dwelling
Thinking of the days of yore
I was startled by a knocking
Gentle knocking at my door
It was brother Harris, postman
With his mailbag, nothing more.

In his hand he held a postal
Which I seized with glad delight.
But alas, my joy was ended
I must read, or else recite
At the coming village social
At Bull's Bridge on Tuesday night.

Of the Socials in your village
I've attended only three
But that postal said do something
So the thought occurred to me
That I would tell of village socials

That we have held up here before
In the year of 'ninety-seven
Only that and nothing more.

First we met with Mr. Spooner
Where we met in time of old
In the balmy days of springtime
When the weather wasn't cold.
It was said that few attended
Though 'twas sounded o'er and o'er
That is all I know about it
Only that, and nothing more.

Next we met with Brother Newton
At his home so near the sky
Where 'twas said by men of olden
That the turkeys used to fly.
Here we talked of Paul and Silas
And of corn that wouldn't pop.
Of the place we ought to plant it
If we wanted half a crop.

And then we had a game
It was a blind affair
Where we looked and smelled and handled
A lot of things both round and square.
And then they gave me something
I dropped it on the floor
To me it smelled and tasted
Just like dirt and nothing more.

When the Social next was held
It was such a stormy night
That the people couldn't get there
But we knew the place was right.

That the rain came down in torrents
And the mighty winds did roar

Was the cause so few attended
Only that and nothing more.

Then another one was held
This time in Gaylordsville
It was appointed at the home
Of Paine and Underhill.
The blind they fed the blind
The corn was on the floor
Because they couldn't find their mouths
Only that, and nothing more.

We heard of Mary's little lamb
Sam Seldon's William goat
And we tried to tell each other
Who some authors were that wrote,
Then we had a doughnut contest
We ate them to the core
When out swung the two big buttons
Only that, and nothing more.

Again we met with Mr. Spooner
This time we were all there
We thought to fill the house
But there was room to spare.
The girls were shy and careful
When they heard the ancient lore
That's the reason few were kissing
Only that, and nothing more.

Our host, he called, we followed on
And then to our surprise
Upon a table in the room
A mammoth cake did rise.
In it a penny, button, ring
Alas, that lonely store
I fear that George will only find
The ring and nothing more.

Thus we met, our friends and neighbors
In the year that has just passed.
May our socials of this year
Be as pleasant as in last.
But we say now once for all
As we've said so oft before
That we'll never eat a doughnut
On a string - no, never more.

An annual event was the Sunday School picnic. Though arranged by the Sunday School, it was actually a community affair. It was held after haying time and before time to cut corn so the farmers would take a day off to go, as it was attended by the whole family. It was sometimes held locally, on Liberty Hill or Cedar Hill, or sometimes held at Bull's Bridge, Lovers Leap, or occasionally at Lake Hammersley in N.Y. State.

With the coining of the auto, the picnics were held farther away. Putnam Park was a favorite spot, as were Lake Waramaug and Lake Quassapaug. In later years interest in the picnics by the adults lessened, and they became mostly a children's affair. Finally, around 1965, they were discontinued.

There have been baseball teams in Gaylordsville from time to time that have provided a lot of entertainment for the baseball fans in the community.

An early team called themselves the Imperials and was playing teams from New Milford and other nearby areas in 1905. Included on this team were Edward Honan, Fremont Hall, Frank Ward, William Thomas, Curtis Hall, Charles Talbot, Nat Ashman, Thomas Austin, Howard Hepburn, Steve Joyce, and Matt Ween. The games were played on a field south of what is now Route 55, sometimes called West Street. The daughter of one of the players recalls going to one of the games wearing a new panama hat, hanging it on a convenient bush while she watched the game. Somebody else had come to the game on a horse. After the game it was discovered that the horse had eaten the hat.

Another team was formed in the late 1920's with Charles and Theodore Jones as the 'battery', catcher and pitcher. This team used one of the river lots a short distance south of the bridge. Seats were built for the spectators and games were played there for several years.

Next a team was formed with Harry Wells as manager. Their games were played on a field behind the Tom Thumb Cabins, between Route 7 and Gaylord Road. This team joined an area league, and to improve its performance used some players from other towns. After a time the New Milford team disbanded and the Gaylordsville team moved there, much to the dismay of the local baseball fans. This was the last baseball team organized in Gaylordsville.

In 1949 a softball team was formed by the fire department and games were played on a field across from the Gaylordsville Garage. The team soon became a separate unit, though it was still sponsored by the department for a time. It eventually became the Gaylordsville Softball Association and a member of a league. Lights were installed on the field so the games could be played at night. There were not many lighted fields in the league so most of the games were played at Gaylordsville. The Association flourished for several years, then interest in softball declined and the field became idle. To make sure the field would always be available, both for recreation and their carnival, the Fire Department bought it and still maintains it as a park.

The Gaylordsville Historical Society

The Gaylordsville Historical Society was formed as an outcome of the planning of Gaylordsville's 250th anniversary celebration held in 1975. Several members of the anniversary committee felt there should be a permanent organization to work towards the preservation of Gaylordsville's history and artifacts. They felt it was also important that the organization should encourage the preservation and restoration of historic buildings and sites. John Flynn Sr., the Gaylordsville historian, organized the society in December 1975. It took nearly two years to wade through all of the "red tape" necessary to become a non-profit organization. The Internal Revenue Service, the state of Connecticut and the town of New Milford granted the society non-profit status and thus, donations to the historical society became tax deductible. The initial officers of the society were, John

Flynn, Sr.; President, George Atkins; Vice president, Barbara Thorland; Secretary, and Mary Jane Williamson; Treasurer.

Since its inception, the society has played an important part in the community. Christmas in Gaylordsville is a prime example of this, partnering with other civic and religious groups to celebrate the Christmas season. There is an open house at the Little Red Schoolhouse with refreshments, a Gaylordsville United Methodist Church fair, a gala open house and arts and crafts fair at Merwinsville Hotel, the Ladies' Auxiliary and volunteer fire department ham dinner, followed by the lighting of the community Christmas tree. The Gaylordsville Historical Society offers memorabilia such as ornaments, postcards and note cards depicting historical sites and picture reprints.

A scholarship, in the memory of Alan S. Farnham, was initiated in 1997. Lt. Farnham, who attended the one room schoolhouse in Gaylordsville, died in combat in Vietnam. Applicants must be a Gaylordsville resident who is a graduating senior and lives within the Gaylordsville Fire District. The following residents have been recipients of this award:

Jeff Stock, New Milford High School, 1997
Michelle Dahl, Nonnewaug High School, 1998
Jared Russell, New Milford High School, 1999
Veena Panduranga, New Milford High School, 2000
Kathryn Martin, New Milford High School, 2001
Allison Demers, New Milford High School, 2002
Kevin Barry, New Milford High School, 2003
Deirdre Mertens, New Milford High School, 2004
Nathaniel Borneman, New Milford High School, 2005
Laura King, New Milford High School, 2006
Carly King, New Milford High School, 2007
Ashley Grenier, New Milford High School, 2008
Ian Smith, New Milford High School, 2009
Christopher Fuchs, New Milford High School, 2010
Brad Ness, New Milford High School, 2011
Nathan Jejer, Nonnewaug High School, 2012
Lindsay Hull, New Milford High School, 2013
John Vazquez, New Milford High School, 2014
Eric Vazquez, New Milford High School 2016

In December of 1997, the Gaylordsville Historical Society took ownership of Brown's Forge from the New Milford Historical Society. This change in ownership ensured that the forge will forever remain in Gaylordsville. Mr. Alan Dodd was named the first curator of Brown's Forge and held that position until his death in 1999. In 2002 a flagpole and plaque, with the following inscription, was dedicated:

> *"This flagpole is dedicated in loving memory to the first president of the Gaylordsville Historical Society, John D. Flynn, whose foresight and dedication made possible the opening of Brown's Forge to the public, and to Alan Dodd, Jack Dodd and James Dolan, long-time member volunteers of the Gaylordsville Historical Society, for their countless hours of volunteerism at the forge."*

In January, 1999 the Historical Society launched its website on the internet. The site, www.gaylordsville.org, has received numerous visits from people throughout the world and has been a very convenient way of keeping in touch with residents who have left the area. Also in the summer of 1999, the Historical Society organized a "Schoolhouse Reunion" where over 100 former students and their families, along with two former teachers, attended the day-long festivities.

Currently, the society has over 100 paid memberships, holds an annual picnic and publishes a yearly membership newsletter. The current officers are, Richard Kosier; President, Barbara Thorland; Secretary, and Celeste Bellemare; Treasurer.

UNUSUAL PEOPLE

Gaylordsville, as does nearly every community, had its share of unusual people that either lived in or passed through the village. One of these, of course, was the Leather Man, who probably visited every community in the area. He passed from town to town, saying nothing and harming no one. The characteristic that set him apart from the hundreds of other vagabonds, pack peddlers and wanderers roaming the northeast in the late 1800's was his clothing. His garb consisted of a heavy leather jacket, leather pants, leather hat and leather shoes with wooden soles. After his death, some curious folk weighed his jacket and found it to tip the scales at about sixty pounds. He traveled a distinct route from the Hudson River in New York, across Connecticut to the Connecticut River, then south to Long Island Sound. On reaching the Sound, he moved east to Norwalk before heading inland back to the Hudson. This was his cycle, a total of about 365 miles. He walked it over and over again for thirty-one years, until his death in 1889. Most amazing of all was the Leatherman's dedication to punctuality. His route took him thirty-four days; no more, no less. Trainmen said they could set their watches by him. People who gave him handouts along the way would mark off the thirty-fourth day on their calendars as "Leatherman's Day." He first appeared one day in 1865. He spoke to no one, perhaps because he was painfully shy or because he did not understand English. On one of his visits he stopped for food at a home where a French woman was employed. Her name was Ann Curry, and she was very much interested in him, looking at him closely while he was there. After he left she said she was sure he was her son, John, whom she had not seen in years. He slept off the road in rock caves and homemade shelters and ate only what was given to him and refused work when it was offered. Only once in his thirty-one years of travel was he known to have strayed off schedule, during the blizzard of 1888. The wind and snow were so tremendous that it virtually closed down the city of New York for days. The people along the Leatherman's trail justifiably feared that he had not survived. But he had weathered the great storm in a shelter in Southington, Connecticut. Old age and the thousands of miles of walking finally brought the old Leatherman to the end of his journey. His body was found on March 24, 1889, near a farm in Pleasantville, New York. He was so famous that he rated a front-page obituary in the New York Sun and the Hartford Times.

Another man who passed through quite often in the late 1800's was Isaac Thorn Chatterton, who reportedly had been quite wealthy until an unfortunate experience affected his mind. On some of his visits he thought he was taking the census, and asked all sorts of questions of anyone who would listen. All of his extra clothing and possessions were carried inside the lining of his overcoat. He sometimes stayed overnight with Amos Brown, and refused to retire for the night until he had prayers with the family. If he was in the village on Sunday he attended church, and during prayers stood facing the wall.

Probably the most familiar character was Walker Prindle. When he was a small boy, his father and mother went west in a horse-drawn wagon. He did not want to go, and when they were ready to start, he hid until they finally left without him. He usually wore a pair of coveralls made of bed ticking, and in summer, a sun bonnet. He made his living doing odd jobs and collecting rags to sell. He always carried a basket for hand-outs and would sing if asked to, though he always apologized for his voice. He somehow obtained snapshots of himself to sell to anyone who wanted to buy one. He sometimes traveled around with two dolls, dressed in bright colors and would show them to people for two cents a look. Once he went to the parsonage and frightened the minister's wife. She thought he had a coffin, as the box he carried was shaped like one. He lived to be an old man and died at the New Milford Town Farm.

Another visitor was John Brennon, better known as "Pick Penny". He usually preferred the larger towns, however, where he might find someone to buy him a drink. Still another man was called "Old June" because that is when he always showed up. His name was Bradshaw, and he was always dressed in rags with pieces of carpet wrapped around his feet.

Perhaps the most unusual person who came through Gaylordsville was the woman with the dogs. She came through every spring, sometimes with as many as twelve dogs, all tied on a rope. Her name was Lonsy Witham and she came from Massachusetts, where she raised the dogs. In the spring she started walking with them to Long Island, where she sold them to bird hunters. Wherever she spent the night she had to sleep in the shed or barn with the dogs or they would howl all night and be too tired to travel the next day. When they started out in the morning, the dogs would nearly pull her off her feet. She seemed to be a well-educated person. She said when her husband was alive, he was a lumberman in the woods and kept the dogs for protection. The last time she came through Gaylordsville, she had young dogs in a baby carriage.

A local woman with unusual habits was Charlotte Gaylord, second wife of John Gaylord. Sometimes called a religious fanatic, she nearly always carried a cross with her. She attended church regularly, but if the minister said something she did not agree with, she would get right up and argue the matter. She usually did her baking and housework at night and roamed about the village during the day. She was killed by a train at Austin's crossing. Some people said that she stepped in front of it deliberately. The cross she carried, or one just like it, was used to mark her grave.

In later years Gaylordsville was the home of a once noted woman, though she lived in seclusion for many years. Known here as Mrs. Chandler, she was actually Florence Maybrick, who had received a guilty verdict in a famous murder trial in England. It was widely believed that her husband was James Maybrick, also known as "Jack The Ripper". James Maybrick was the unfortunate victim of arsenic poisoning. After serving her term in prison, she came to America, and eventually to Gaylordsville in 1917. She was employed as a housekeeper by Miss Henrietta Banwell, but soon left that position and had a small cottage built on Old Stone Road. Here she lived in almost complete seclusion, coming to the village only for groceries and mail. She acquired a houseful of cats, and bought two quarts of milk a day for them. She had a very small income and sometimes was unable to pay for her groceries, but always received what she needed anyway.

Florence Maybrick's cottage on Old Stone Road

Her true identity was learned by Mrs. Thomas Austin, to whom Mrs. Chandler had given a dress. In looking over the dress, Mrs. Austin discovered a label with the name "Florence Maybrick" sewed in one shoulder. She told her husband, and they decided to keep the discovery a secret, which they did until after Mrs. Chandler's death. The road the cottage was on continued on through the woods to a point near South Kent School. She became acquainted with some of the boys and teachers, who made sure she always had enough to eat and wood for her stove. Before she died she made a written request to Mr. Bartlett, the headmaster, asking that her funeral service be held in the school chapel, and that she be buried on the school grounds. When she died, on October 23, 1941 her requests were granted. She was then seventy-nine, and had lived in Gaylordsville for twenty-one years. No one else ever used the cottage, and it is now in ruins.

Another unusual person was Jan Pol, who was born in 1894 in Poland and came to Gaylordsville in 1922, according to his book "Jan Pol, The Passage Of My Life." He lived on the corner of what is now Riverview Road and South Kent Road, with his wife, Josephine. The building was built by George Ward, who sold groceries and meat and subsequently sold the building to Jan Pol. (NOTE: His name is spelled Jan in this book and the name was pronounced as "John Pole.") Mr. Pol conducted a meat market in the building and added living quarters in the rear of the store. He started selling second-hand articles and antiques. The building was partly destroyed by fire on November 16, 1968, but was rebuilt. He was sure it was the work of vindictive villagers who threw a Molotov cocktail through the window of the glassed-in front porch. He and his wife adopted a little girl in the late 1940's and she would appear with him at the Danbury Fair, where he was garbed as the "Old Prospector," complete with burros. It is remembered that her name was Leona, although in the book he refers to her as "the girl." As time went on, Leona became pregnant and when she delivered a daughter, Catherine, the state took the child away. It was not known for sure who the father was. A heartbroken Jan Pol built a monument on the riverbank across from his home with a sign that read "I am Catherine Dessareau Pol. This building is my memory. I was born in a hospital and two and one-half days later the Child Welfare Department kidnapped me, saying "It is not fit that I grow here." Mr. Pol was very interested in the establishment of a fire department in Gaylordsville and extended his help to the fire department by paying for materials used in the building of the initial firehouse, according to his book. He was an eccentric in many ways, but by all accounts, an honest and decent person.

Clarence Evans, the renowned photographer of Gaylordsville, was born in November, 1870. He was the husband of Elma Bidwell Evans. Clarence received his first camera for Christmas in 1888. He started taking pictures in 1889 all over Connecticut, documenting everything he saw. He did not depict the most sophisticated subjects but rather took pictures of everyday life and people. He had a way of portraying children with captivating facial expressions, sometimes holding a toy and always looking very natural. It was noted that Mr. Evans took a painfully long time to pose people, as in the case of wedding and other group pictures. This might account for the slightly pained look on the faces of some of the people in these types of photographs. Clarence Evans' original glass-plate negatives were given to the Gaylordsville Historical Society by Mrs. Mabel Honan. She and her husband, Tommy Honan, had purchased the Evans' home in 1955. A number of photographs by Clarence Evans are now on view in the museum at the Merwinsville Hotel. Many of the pictures in this book are those of Clarence Evans, who died in January, 1954. (Some of this information was supplied by Mr. Charles Bidwell of New York City, nephew of Elma Bidwell Evans.)

One of the most beloved residents of Gaylordsville will always be Manuel Williamson. His real name was Abraham Emanuel Williamson, but to everyone around here, he was just plain "Manuel." He was born in Norway on April 6, 1892, and came to Gaylordsville in 1908. He worked on the Gabe Thompson farm. In 1914 he went to work at Remington Arms in Bridgeport. After World War I service in the Army, he worked for a time in Danbury and then opened the Gaylordsville Garage on September 1, 1923. He was one of the longest continuous Mobil dealers in the east and was honored at the Mobil Dealers' Convention in Las Vegas in 1972. During World War II he organized the Gaylordsville Home Guard and was Chief Air Raid Warden for the Gaylordsville sector. He was a charter member of the Gaylordsville Volunteer Fire Department and a member of Gaylordsville's Wemanesa Grange. Gaylordsville's first fire truck was kept in Manuel's barn on Gaylord Road, across from the garage. The barn has been converted into a cozy home owned by his son, David and wife, Mary Jane Dodd Williamson. In 1972, on the occasion of his 80th birthday, Manuel was honored at a celebration of over 500 people who came from near and far to greet him and to say "thank you" for his unfailing services to his community and travelers passing through town. He was always cheerfully ready to help in any way he could, day or night, from providing wrecker service or car repair or advice, to taking service men to the train and/or picking them up from the train on their return home, as well as in countless other ways. At his birthday celebration, he recalled the time a farmer called and said he needed Manuel's wrecker for "a little job." When Manuel arrived, he found a cow in a well and promptly went to work to remove said cow in time for the night milking. He also recalled a few fast races to the hospital. He will long be remembered for his greeting of "Good Morning," no matter the time of day, to folks arriving for gas, car repair, or just plain advice about something. Manuel passed away on December 7, 1973. Funeral services were held in New Milford. When the funeral procession passed through Gaylordsville, on the way to his burial in Morningside Cemetery, the bells of the Gaylordsville United Methodist Church tolled in his honor, a fitting tribute to one of Gaylordsville's most memorable citizens.

PART 2

HISTORIC HOUSES OF GAYLORDSVILLE

Several homes still standing were built or lived in by Gaylords. In the southern part of the village the first house on Gaylord Road after crossing the town line from Sherman is the McGoldrick house. Legend tells us this house was built by a Gaylord, but there are no records to show if this was really the case. One of the unique features of this house is that it has five fireplaces. There are two on the main floor for heat and one for cooking. On the basement level there is one fireplace for heat and one for the summer cooking. The first mention of this house is in town records of 1817, when David Bostwick sold it to Derrick Tibbetts. Next it went to John C. Preston, Henry Osborn, Drake Woolsey, John McGoldrick and William McGoldrick. Mrs. Margaret McGoldrick lived in the family home until her death. The William McGoldrick's son, Bill, recently passed away. His wife, Phyllis, still lives there.

The next house on Gaylord Road, at the foot of Old Stilson Road, is part of the original James F. Morrissey farm, and is the only brick house in the community. It was the home of Albert Gaylord. The original part of the house was made entirely of local materials, the bricks being made of native clay and baked in a kiln nearby. The doorsills are of native marble, and have become hollowed out from years of wear. The wooden section on the back was added later. Following the death of the Morrissey sisters, the place was sold to Robert Martin, who sold it in 1988 to Mr. and Mrs. Peter Skinner.

The next house to the north was also owned by the Morrisseys. It was built by David Gaylord, who ran a mill nearby, It was purchased by the Knapps, and is still called the Knapp house by some of the older residents. The Morrisseys bought it and used it as a home for their hired man as long as the farm was operating. It is now a two-family home owned by the Robert Martin family and is rented to others.

There were several Williams in the Gaylord family over the years, and one of them built the large house south of the school. It was later purchased by Ebenezer Sanford, who was there in 1854. The next owner was Martin Hungerford, who built and operated a large tobacco warehouse next to it. Later owners were Thomas Silver, and Norris Wildman. It has undergone extensive remodeling and at one time housed a deluxe restaurant, known as the Brookhill Manor. It was owned by a Mrs. Levintritt, then the Noel Castle family and is now owned by Betsy and Simon Clark and family.

The house north of the school, east of the road, was built by Daniel Gaylord in 1801. The part of the foreground, with the porch, was built much later. This house remained in the Gaylord family long after all of the others had new owners. The last to live here was William Gaylord. When he died in 1945, Gaylordsville, for the first time since its first settlers arrived two hundred and twenty years earlier was without a Gaylord. The house was owned by S. Pelham Thayer, the George Bossers family and is now owned by Mr. & Mrs. Duke Nelson.

Diagonally across the road was a house built by Ebenezer Gaylord and his wife and he ran a tavern there. According to local lore, Mrs. Gaylord was shot at by Tories, but they missed. Later the house burned down and a new one was built by Nathan Gaylord, probably in the early 1800's. George was the last Gaylord to live here. This house, too, shows signs of extensive remodeling. It now has thirteen rooms and three fireplaces, one with a brick oven. Later owners were Gabriel Thompson, Fred Dennis, Nick Edmonds, Nelson Edmonds, John Mullen, and presently it is owned by Dayle and Charles Elsesser.

The next house to the north, east of the road, was the second house built in Gaylordsville. The main part of the house was built in 1729 by Aaron, son of William Gaylord, the first settler. It was the birthplace and lifetime home of Truman Gaylord, who died in 1888. Later owners were Hallock, Soule, Mr.& Mrs. John Cornwell, and Joseph Cass. Mrs. John Cornwell (Bessie Cornwell was the long-time teacher at the Gaylord School just down the road from her home.) The rear section of this house was damaged by fire, but was repaired and the house has been extensively remodeled. It is now owned by Mr. & Mrs. Fred Cass.

A little farther north, west of the road, is the former home of Joseph Gaylord. A map of 1853 shows it occupied by S. Levi, and in 1867 by C.E. Conkrite. More recent owners were William Leviness and Robert Cornell. It is presently owned by Richard Cass. The second floors in the two sections are not accessible to each other, and can be reached only by separate stairways from the ground floor.

On Route 7, directly across the street from the Methodist Parsonage, is the former home of Charles Gaylord, the artist. Part of this house was originally on the other side of the road, a little to the south, and was moved around 1860 and joined with another building to form the present structure. It was occupied by a Miss Gaylord until about 1890. It was later purchased by Mr. and Mrs. Curtis Hall and was their home for many years. The Meissners next owned it for a few years, then Walter Arndt. It most recently was owned by Kay and Al Stietzel, where they raised their children, Jean and John. Following their deaths, the home is now owned by Dimitria Stefanopoulos.

Across the river, next to the store, is the house built by Peter Gaylord in 1805. He lived there until he died in 1879 at the age of ninety-five. His son, John, who took over the store, may have lived there after that. It was later occupied for a time by the Potters, then by the Thorps. It was purchased by Mrs. Peterson and her daughter, both of whom were nurses. It was then owned by Mrs. Mary Sanford. On the death of Mrs. Sanford the house was sold to a succession of owners and presently is owned by Mr. and Mrs. James Dalzell and family.

On the South Kent Road the Anna Koster house was the home of John Gaylord. It was probably built by a Merwin, as the 1853 map shows it belonging to the estate of a Merwin. Mr. Gaylord bought it soon after that and was still there in 1867. It was later purchased by Henry Disbrow. After his death it became the property of his wife, who later became Mrs. Joseph Duryea. It was purchased by Miss Koster in 1947. There are now nine rooms, a large kitchen on the back having been removed. It is presently the home of Alisyn and Daniel Hamilton and family.

The next house on South Kent Road was built by A.N. Canfield around 1840, and was later purchased by S.W. Bailey. John Hepburn married one of the Bailey girls and they became owners of the house. Nellie Hepburn married a Northrup and it became the Northrup house. It was purchased by John Flynn in 1955. There are ten rooms and a full attic that contains a large, built-in carpet loom. Following John Flynn's death in 1985, the Peter Flynn family resided there. Presently it is the home of Aline Flynn and family.

Next is a house built in 1836 by William K. Evans. Originally there were eight rooms, but four more were added later. The hearthstone for the large fireplace and brick oven was brought from the Roxbury Hill quarries. It is ten feet long, three and a half feet wide, and ten inches thick. Clarence Evans, the renowned photographer, and his wife, Elma Bidwell Evans lived in this house. The house stayed in the Evans family until 1955, when it was purchased by Thomas (Tommy) and Mabel Honan. The house was owned by Ellen and Ted Berson, both now deceased.

A little farther on is the house once owned by the renowned artist, Sascha Maurer and his wife, Olga. The barn on this property, now used as a garage and studio, was built in 1825, probably by a Camp. It was built to live in and has a fireplace. The house was built a few years later, either by a Camp or Canfield, who followed as owner. Later owners were H.O. Ward, Peter Boinay, who married Lottie Ward, then Miss Smith, George Ward and Sascha Maurer, who bought it in 1946. The house has eight rooms, but there is evidence that partitions dividing smaller rooms have been removed. Three fireplaces are located around a central chimney. Following the death of her husband, Mrs. Maurer moved to smaller quarters and the house is presently owned by Linda and Jim Hart.

On the corner of South Kent Road and Grove Road stood a large house built around 1860 by Merwin Waller. The Waller family owned it and ran the dairy farm until 1941, when Fred Waller sold it to George Strid, who continued the farming. There are fourteen large rooms and two fireplaces. The former Strid home burnt down in the early 1980's and a smaller house was rebuilt in the same location by Jane Strid Morris and her husband, Sandy. The home is presently owned by Barbara Richardson and her sons, Patrick and Alex.

Not far from the west end of Grove Road is a house with an interesting past. This house once stood in Brooklyn, New York. In 1914 new approaches were being built to the Brooklyn Bridge, and this house was in the way. Andrew Karcher was in Brooklyn at that time and bought it, had it taken down, brought to Gaylordsville, and put up again. It had been a three-story house, but only two stories, with nine rooms, were put up here. Andrew's son, George, sold it to the Coreys in 1971, who in turn sold it to the Fitzgeralds in 1973. It is presently owned by the Carson family.

On Route Seven, a short distance south of Grove Road stands a house built in the early 1800's by John Paine. Title to the property passed on to James Paine, then to his son, John. Later owners were Harry Antman, Garrett Taylor, Phyllis Dodd, and Allen Ade, who operated a dog kennel and Balmoral Pet Cemetery on the property. The house has a large living room with a low exposed-beam ceiling. The house is still in the Ade family.

On Riverview Road the first house beyond the stores was owned by Mrs. Joseph Corey. Long known as the Barlow house, it was built around 1860 by Bradley Barlow and was the home of Alexander Barlow, a longtime storekeeper and postmaster. It was later inherited by Mrs. Nellie Northrup, who eventually sold it to Frank Beach. It was owned by his daughter, Mrs. Corey, who rented it to others. Originally a large one-family home, it has been used for many years as a two-family home, and was occupied by the Kenneth Posts and Gladys Williamson. It is now owned by Beverly Marden.

A little farther east on Riverview Road is probably the oldest house in that part of the village. It was owned briefly by Truman Gaylord, who bought a half interest in it from a Fairchild on March 31, 1827. The other half interest was purchased on April 2, 1837, by Northrup Kellogg. Robert Kellogg bought it in 1869, and Charles Pomeroy in 1900. Since then it has been owned by Helen Leonhard, Anna Koster, Edward Winchester, Frieda Goodell, and Peter Flynn, who bought it in 1963. It is a seven-room house with a fireplace and brick oven. It was owned at one time by Dan Coppolo and is presently owned by Zoe Vandermeer.

Across the road is the Honan house which first appears on an 1867 map under the name of 0. Warner. It was purchased by Edward Honan in 1900 for $1,900.00. There are three fireplaces downstairs and one up. Two of them are so small that it seems unlikely that anything other than charcoal could have been burned in them. The fireplace with the brick oven has two cranes in it instead of the usual one. The small building in back was originally down the bank and was a slaughterhouse. The home was once owned by Lawrence Honan, brother of Tommy Honan. Following Lawrence Honan's death, the home was purchased by Mr. and Mrs. Joseph Koch. Mr. Koch's widow, Kathleen, lived there for a time. The house is presently owned by Kristin and Daniel Ruman.

This house was built by William (Will) Roberts in 1906. Mr. Roberts also built the F. Luis Mora home on Cedar Hill Road and the Willowbrook Creamery building. Will Roberts married Emma Buckingham. Their daughter, Marjorie, married Paul Richmond of New Milford. Will Roberts died in 1930. His widow kept the family home until 1943, when it was sold to Henrietta Banwell, who was instrumental in bringing Florence Maybrick (of Jack the Ripper fame) to Gaylordsville. Miss Banwell sold the home to the Haenel family. It was then sold to the George Steinman family, then Mark Mazer, and now the present owner is Ilene Deutsch.

This house is located about a hundred yards off Riverview Road next to the Womenshenuck Book. An early owner was Morris Barnes, who operated a grist mill and plaster mill nearby. William Talbot bought it and built a foundry near the mill. The next owner was Bradley Barlow, who added a cider mill to the complex. Around 1905 it was purchased by the New Milford Power Company, who had plans to build a dam about three miles down the river and flood the area. The dam was never built, and a succession of company employees rented the house, the last being George Parker. Charles Pomeroy finally bought it and made it into a two-family house that was rented to various tenants. After his death it was sold to the Peter Prange, who had kennels there. The house has had a succession of owners and presently is the home of Mr. and Mrs. Roger Malmberg.

At the intersection of Riverview Road and River Road stands a house built by Jackson J. Graves. The date on the cellar wall is 1867, but a house appears on a map of 1853 at this location. Originally it had twelve rooms but removing partitions has reduced the number to ten. It was purchased by Charles Pomeroy and later became the home of Henry Pomeroy. As a two-family house it was the home of Mr. & Mrs. Martin Fuchs and Mrs. Marian Cramer. It is now owned by the George Haase family. The late George Haase was the driving force behind the Merwinsville Hotel Restoration and was its first president. His wife, Geraldine, and her family continue to live here.

The house of the Superintendent of the Willow Brook Creamery was built in 1899. After the creamery went out of business, the house was owned by the Wesley Pomeroy family, and then the property was sold to Elmer Carlson. The next owner was Mrs. Aurella Dann, who sold the house to Rosemary and Jerry Nahley in 1970. The Nahley's still own this house, called "Creamery Hill." They were the owners and proprietors of Honan's Store for 23 years. It has just been sold to Audrey Supple.

This house on Brown's Forge Road was probably built as a barn, but by 1853 had been converted into a house by B. Benedict. By 1867 it had been purchased by F. Weaver. It was later owned by Bryce Weaver, and finally by Newton Weaver until it was purchased by Frank Piliero. The original part of the house had eight rooms that were remodeled into six. Three rooms were added on the back. The old chimney that undoubtedly had fireplaces has been removed. Frank Piliero's widow, Helene, continued to live in the family home until her death in 2014. Her daughter, Susan Mullins, resides there presently.

Farther north on Brown's Forge Road, about a quarter of a mile beyond the blacksmith shop is a house occupied in 1853 by H. Merwin. By 1867 it had been taken over by B. Benedict, who had a blacksmith shop on Mud Pond Road where the Browns learned the trade. Sometime after that a man named Fitzpatrick lived there. He decided to get rid of his wife by pushing her into the fireplace. His plan was successful as she died from the burns, but he spent the rest of his life in an insane asylum. The house was purchased by the Honans, who operated the farm until they sold it to Frank Beach, who also ran the farm. In the early 1940's it was purchased by the Dikes, who sold it to the Goodales. It is presently owned by the Soldner family.

A few hundred feet before Brown's Forge Road joins the South Kent Road, a large house sits near the edge of a former cranberry marsh. It was built before 1853, when it was occupied by Merwin Waller. The next owner was J. Varney, who was followed by Edward Austin. It was owned by the Austins for many years, until the death of Thomas Austin. It was occupied for a time by Donald Boerum, Howard Cox, and several other families. Presently it is owned by Kerith and Marvin Putnam.

On the South Kent Road about a quarter of a mile south of the Kent town line is a house that was the Fanton home for many years. When they sold the house and farm, they kept a small plot for a family cemetery. The Edeens bought the place and operated the farm, also keeping it for many years It is now owned by Andrew Sternweiss, who recently passed away, but the home still remains in the family.

Even closer to the Kent line is this house that as far back as 1853 was the home of Edward Hallock. Mr. Hallock was the chef at the station hotel and eventually moved closed to his job, selling the house to O.W. Marcy. It was owned by Leroy Lane, who had lovely rose gardens on the property, and following his death has had several owners. It is now owned by the Anderson/Vogt family.

On the South Kent Road south of Brown's Forge Road is a house that has 1798 over the door. For years it was connected with the Austin farm and was probably used by the hired men. In 1867 W. Lee was there, and in 1874 J. Anson, Later occupants were the Parsons and Bessie Austin Burr. It remained in the Austin family until purchased by the McCormicks in the late 1930's, and was owned by Grace Skyer McCormick, and presently by Kenneth Skyer.

There are two old houses on Old Stone Road. The one pictured above was built before 1853, when it was occupied by R. Canfield. By 1867, and for many years afterward, it was owned by the Stone family, for whom the road was named. It was later owned by Andrew Thorp, and more recently by the Chambers, who sold it to James Cornelius. The most recent owner is Christine Sinclair.

Farther along Old Stone Road is a house once owned by Carl Irwin. The house was purchased from the Straight family by Mr. and Mrs. John Roche in 1850. In the early 1920's, it was purchased by Miss Elizabeth Irwin and Miss Katherine Anthony for a summer retreat. Miss Irwin's adopted son, Carl Irwin and family lived there for several years. The present owners are Mr. and Mrs. Barry Marcus.

This is the former Waller District schoolhouse, which is a private home, owned by Maureen and Richard Utera.

This house is on Waller Road, next to the brook. From 1867 to 1888, at least, it was owned by D. Ditton, before being purchased by Ed Hallock. Later it was rented by various tenants, among them the Rocks, and the Pennys. When it was purchased by George and Sherry Zabriskie, it was in poor repair, but was completely restored. It was owned by Richard Vom Lehn. The next owner, Fred Voelpel, recently sold the house to Jeffrey and Beverly Pierpaoli.

Circa 1796 house is located across from Browns Forge and includes over 7 acres of property. It was owned for many years by Alan Himelich and lately by the Lee family.

Hardly visible from any road, this house was owned by Reverend Paul Weed. It was built around 1860, near the Womenshenuck Brook, by T.G. Bailey. At one time Matt Kilcourse, a railroad section foreman, lived there, possibly as a boarder. He killed himself by jumping head first into the well. Sylvester Hepburn became owner of the place, probably because he was a descendant of the Baileys. He was there most of his life, doing some farming and some carpentry work. It was then purchased by Reverend Weed, who lived there until his death. It was then the home of Dallas and Katie Reed and their family. Following the death of Dallas, Katie continues to make it her home.

The first four houses on Route 55 all seem to have been built within a few years. The first one was the home of Mrs. Wooster in 1867. The next owners were the Stones and then the Deckers. For several years it was occupied by Judge Bryan during the summer. Mrs. Elizabeth Decker's daughter, Nancy Decker Humphreys, lived in this house until her death, and the house is presently owned by her son, Peter.

This house, directly across the road from the former Levko Siloti home, was built by John Gaylord, possibly as early as 1855. It was occupied by John Dolan and his wife, Maria Fitzsimon Dolan. He bought it from Mr. Gaylord in 1872 and sold it to his son, Dr. John A. Dolan, in 1902. On the death of Dr. Dolan in 1916, it became the property of his wife, Gertrude, who later married a Millspaugh. Andrew Blom bought it in 1924 and owned it until 1945 when it was sold to Albert Miller. The Millers and Furnsides were there until 1961, when it was purchased by Page Hunt. Herman Jacot bought it in 1966 and sold it to John Brothers in 1968, who sold it to Mrs. Jean Voris in 1973, and it is presently the home of John and Gladys Roswell.

In 1853 this house, the second one on Route 55, was sold by G.W. Morse to Eric Helsten. There was a grist mill and a tannery included with the property, and Mr. Helsten operated both of them. He died in 1903 and his son-in-law, Charles Evans, took over the property and continued to operate the grist mill. Burton Booth bought it in 1916 and kept the mill going until 1926. In that year he sold it to the Cavanaugh's and the mill was torn down. Mark and Fran Dingee bought the house around 1950, and sold it to Levko Siloti, in 1956. It was then sold to Stephen Strinecka, then to Mr. and Mrs. Jeff Gambino. It is presently the home of Nancy Sexton and family.

The next house on Route 55, next to the intersection of Newton Road, is very similar in appearance to the Roswell house. It was also built by John Gaylord, probably by the same carpenter and at about the same time. It was sold to Leman Hendricks as soon as it was completed. Later owners were Kelsey, Benny, Edward Gardner, Mrs. Rogers, and Diane and Carl Myhill. The home is presently owned by Timothy Rogers.

Some of the houses south of the bridge on Route 7 are older than those on Route 55. The first one was owned by Marcus Platt in 1853, and by B. Platt a few years later. The Barnum's lived there for awhile before it was purchased by the Kennedy's around 1902. Anna Kennedy married Charles Walden, and with the coming of Route 7 and increasing traffic, they opened the Walden Tourist Home. Many of their guests returned year after year to spend a weekend or longer in the spacious home. They were in business for over thirty-five years, nearly until their deaths in the mid-1960's. The house was then purchased by the Mitchell's. They kept it until 1973, when it was purchased by Robert Bierbower. It is now owned by a private party and is rented to others.

The next house on Route 7 shows on all the early maps under the name of Marsh, at least until 1888. Later the Potters lived there, after which it was rented to several families over a period of years. After World War II it was purchased by the Baldwins, enlarged and operated as the Gaylordsville Inn. The venture was not very successful, and after a few years the Inn was sold to Frederick Ridolfi, who passed away in September, 2005. Mr. Ridolfi had operated the building as a rest home and subsequently sold the building which continued to be operated as a rest home until it was closed in June, 2006.

On the east side of Route 7, the second house from the former grange hall is one of the older ones in this part of the village. The 1853 map shows it being occupied by T. McConnell, and in 1867 by Mrs. Hurd. A later occupant was Mrs. Kellogg, before it was purchased by Oliver Marcy. George Ward bought it and rented it to Thornton Lane, who was there until 1944. Following the Lanes, the Thomas Dodds were there for several years, after which it was purchased by Warren Buck in 1951. It was later purchased by Edward Burnett and then was owned by Mark and Gail Estabrooks. Although it looks small, it has seven rooms on its three floors. The present owner is Mrs. Sandy Brenner.

The house south of the church was built before 1853 and was owned by the Hallock family for many years. In 1884 it was purchased from Mrs. Hallock by the Methodist Church for use as a parsonage. Many ministers and their families have lived here since that date, some for only one year, others for as long as seven years. The house has seven rooms and a fireplace.

This home was built in 1890, and was owned over the years by Mr. and Mrs. Martin Tomasovski, then Ulrich Wolf, then the Jeter family, then Renee and Bill Wilcox. Presently Bill Wilcox has a Harley-Davidson motorcycle repair shop in the rear of this home. The house is owned by Rae Renee Meerbergen.

This home is about a mile and a half south on Route 7, just south of Straits Rock. In 1853 it was owned by Jabez Covill, who by 1888 had turned it over to his son, Henry. The New Milford Savings Bank acquired it by mortgage, and sold it to George Brague in 1901, who in turn sold it to John Flynn in 1902. Albert Larson bought it in 1915 and sold it back to John Flynn in 1922. While owned by the Flynns, it was the home of Harry Johnson, Harry Wells, and Oscar Miller. It was purchased by John and Mildred Ward in 1944. The house was not originally a salt box, but was given that appearance by an addition put on by the Wards. It is now owned by the Robert Fuller family.

About a quarter of a mile farther south on Route 7, this house was the second one on this site. It was built in 1837 after the first one burned and was almost twice as big as the old cellar over which it was built. The twelve-room house had two fireplaces downstairs, the large one in the kitchen having a brick oven. There was also a fireplace upstairs. The property has been owned by Azariah Howland, Frank Briggs, Abraham Northrup, Ebenezer Sanford, and David Northrup, who sold it to John Flynn in 1867. This lovely old home was demolished for a gravel bank in the 1970's, although the town had been given assurances by the developer John Lobdell that it would not be destroyed.

And now at the beginning of the 21st century, Gaylordsville has evolved from being a village of mostly trades people and farmers to a town that includes people who commute to other places. In the 1980's George Washington Plaza was built with a large C-Town Supermarket and various smaller stores. The supermarket was far too large to be supported by the community and went out of business after a short time. Today that vast space is occupied by Conway Hardwoods, dealers in specialty woods that are shipped all over the country.

The popular Gaylordsville Diner is also in this complex as is the newly located Gaylordsville Post Office, which opened in spacious new quarters in 2006. There is a hair salon, a liquor store and various other small businesses as well as several commercial condos in back of the plaza.

George Washington Plaza

Originally this property was the location of the Valley Appliance Center, sales and service of appliances and televisions, owned by Barbara and Ray Thorland. The property had been in the family since the 1930's. Presently it is the home of Aline Flynn's Hepatica, a treasure filled store of vintage items.

Alfredo's Restaurant is owned by Mimi and Franco Leto. Celebrating 30 years in Gaylordsville, Alfredo's is the local favorite for Italian food and pizza.

The Basket Shop continues to offer a varied line of gifts and baskets and also decorative and household gift items. The former Aaron Seltzer property is now occupied by The Village Farm, which is owned and operated by Lise Goedewaagen. She and her staff grow produce in season and during the winter sell "The Worlds Best Wreaths" and Christmas trees and seasonal decorations.

The Village Farm

INDEX

W

Printed in the United States
By Bookmasters